To the Master Gardener, the Lover of my soul, whose grace had been watering His own eternal seed all along….

Who knew?

Copyright ©☐ 2021

All rights reserved

MerryJo Portell

Behold Thine Enemy...

**And literally get the HELL out of your own way!
What you don't know CAN hurt you!
Living proof that not all who wander are
" lost!"**

Remember, you're not the first one that he has tried to deceive...that story started long ago in the garden with Adam and Eve!

A loud voice will command you to put this book down; a gentle voice will encourage you to embrace it. Both of the voices are fighting for your soul. Only One has won.

You might be a prodigal if….
- *You feel like you're on the outside looking in..*
- *You have abandoned the idea of going to a traditional "church" ...*
- *You're enslaved to an addiction that you've convinced yourself you can't get out of...*
- *You've been sexually, physically, emotionally abused*
- *A recording in your head keeps telling you "it's too late to turn back now" ...*
- *You're suicidal and or depressed, feel abandoned, rejected, financially distraught*
- *You've given up all hope of ever changing*
- *You feel like God is mad at you*
- *You're angry at God for taking someone or something away from you*
- *You mock Christianity*
- *MOST IMPORTANTLY: You accepted Jesus Christ at one time in your life, fully embracing the gospel of your salvation, forgetting that you*

were permanently born into the Father's divine family the moment you believed that Jesus Christ died for your sins, was buried and rose again on the 3rd day imputing His own righteousness in place of yours and will be returning very soon to rapture His church.

Jesus Christ never forfeited His end of the deal, regardless of the distance we've wandered, the gospel of our salvation was never a feeling...it's always been a FACT, a COVENANT that Jesus Christ made with His Father, a COVENANT that nothing or no one has the power to erase; for at that moment in eternity, we passed from spiritual death to spiritual life and our names were permanently recorded in the Lamb's book of life and we were sealed FOREVER!

Amazing isn't it?

And we did absolutely nothing but believe!

Wake up from your slumber, child of God...don't let the enemy put you in a spiritual checkmate. Jesus Christ already won.

It is finished, remember?

FYI...It doesn't matter who or what led you down that wrong road...God's amazing grace allows U-turns. Most importantly...if you're NOT currently a Christian, you WILL very soon be left behind in this world to endure the darkest of nights in the rapidly approaching seven-year tribulation...

1Cor 15:1-4

Why suffer inevitable wrath when Salvation is as simple as the ABC's?

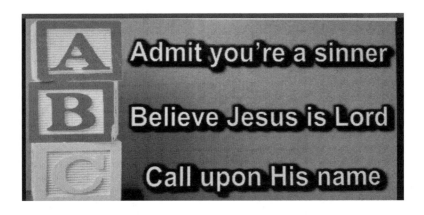

Photo Credit:
JDFarag.org

Hebrews 10:14 For by ONE offering He has perfected FOREVER them that are sanctified.

Religion won't save you! Buddha, Mohammed, Allah can't save you. Church attendance won't! Nor will Mary, dead saints, your rosary, your good works or those of your ancestors.

You can't depend on your luck, your bank account, your status in life or the mask that you're currently wearing to keep you safe. Furthermore, there is nothing" good" in man that by a" formula" or" program" we can even return to. We must be born-again!
There is ONLY one name that saves and ONLY one way to Heaven!
That name is Jesus Christ….
The eternally existing God of Abraham, Isaac and Jacob!!!
What you don't know CAN hurt you, friend! This book isn't as much about getting "lost" people

saved….as it is locating and educating "saved" people getting lost. Being informed, or staying deceived is a choice and that choice, my friend, is a matter of spiritual life or death. Choose wisely!

Table of Contents

Forward: Foul Play

Part 1: Behind enemy lines

Chapter one: Framed
Chapter two: My brother's keeper
Chapter three: Orphans in the storm
Chapter four: Born again at eleven
Chapter five: The rules of engagement
Chapter six: Web of lies

Part 2:   Created crisis

Chapter seven: Behind the mask
Chapter eight: Paranormal Activity/Occult
Chapter nine: Souled out
Chapter ten: Altered states
Chapter eleven: Satan takes the stage
Chapter twelve: Lockdown
Chapter thirteen: Holiday prey

Part 3: Full circle

Chapter fourteen: There's no place like home
Chapter fifteen: Losing my religion
Chapter sixteen: The Great deception
Chapter seventeen: Dead man walking
Chapter eighteen: Who's afraid of the big, bad wolf?
Chapter nineteen: Doubting Thomas
Chapter twenty: A Galilean wedding
Chapter twenty-one: Claiming the spoils
Chapter twenty-two: The rapture

Epilogue: Left behind

****The best way to keep a prisoner
from escaping is to make sure
he never knows he's in prison.

Fyodir Dostoevsky

Behold-(verb)-see, as if for the first time

The word "behold" occurs 1326 times In the King James Version of the bible... To perceive, pay attention, to inspect, examine, to know, Turn one's eyes to, to see about, to have regard for:

No sympathy for the Devil

My, my, what a big mouth God Almighty has redeemed.

My life wasn't as worthless as you made it seem. I pray that every black sheep within the sound of my voice becomes radically loosened from your grip, enabled to make a free choice.

I'll bet you never realized when you bound me up in chains, that my life would be an instrument to spare others from your pain.

I'll bet you never noticed, as you pushed me further into that grave, that my heart was transcribing notes that God in His mercy had saved.

I'll bet it never occurred to you when you tempted me into your land, that God would call me to be an eyewitness and one day take the stand.

I'm almost compelled to thank you, Satan, for pushing me so hard to the ground, for had I not been in the dirt, my Savior's mercy I may not have found.

So, it is in humble adoration, I dedicate each word transcribed within these pages, to the faithful Shepherd of the flock, the Lamb ordained before the ages. The rulers of this world couldn't have known the end of His story…

For if they had known the great mystery of God, they wouldn't have crucified my Lord of glory.

1 Cor 2:7-8

7 But we speak the wisdom of God in a mystery, even the hidden wisdom, which God ordained before the world unto our glory:

8 Which none of the princes of this world knew: for had they known it, they would not have crucified the Lord of glory.

Part one:
Behind Enemy Lines

Forward:

Foul play

How would you respond if someone informed you of an opportunity to turn every wrong you've ever done in your life into a treasured masterpiece? I know it's hard to believe, but it's true.

If life had dealt me a wonderful beginning, perhaps I would've missed this incredible end. Ironically; it was there, in the most painful season of my life that I would learn how to appreciate and eventually cherish the beauty of defeat. I responded to this invitation solely out of desperation, but you certainly don't have to wait until then to receive it.

Humanly speaking, I should be long gone but despite my ignorance and willful resistance, Jesus Christ wielded that glorious plan of *redemption in His hand, denying the enemy permanent access.*

In His infinite wisdom, God Almighty designed every bit of my prodigal lifestyle to one day bring untold glory back to Himself.

Today is that day!

Scary thought that some of us unwittingly spend our entire lives believing lies, subconsciously accepting counterfeit identities, without the slightest clue that we've been framed by an invisible enemy,

To the untold population also suspecting foul play, perhaps this book is exactly what you've been waiting for; evidence that not only confirms your suspicions of foul play but provides a very concrete plan of escape. Listening to someone else's account, often enables us to believe that, beneath our own life's wreckage, a still small voice beckons. It's been said that the pivotal force for change is pain. It was the very key to unlock my life's bolted door. With that same key I was given the wisdom and clarity to behold my enemy and arrest him in his tracks.

I was then asked to write a formal complaint, reporting the facts of my unlawful detention, that you, too, might witness the final verdict. This is my burden of proof; concrete evidence that Justice still prevails in the lives of all who seek true liberty.

My prayer is that you come to the understanding that catching and detaining your suspect relies solely upon your ability to clearly see the Truth and willingly recognize the lies, for it is your responsibility and a great privilege to find out exactly who and what stands in harm's way!

Like any burglar your enemy isn't going to surrender until he's identified and caught. Beloved, Jesus Christ is the only One with the power and authority to detain him. This isn't called a war for nothing and we wouldn't be called soldiers if we weren't expected to fight.

Time as we know it, dear reader is quickly running out, and together we stand at the threshold of His story's final chapter. If you don't believe in His Story, you can bet that your enemy has everything to do with that unbelief….and if you do believe, what is the fruit of that belief? Just for the record, it was never my ambition to write a story about the enemy and you can bet that it isn't by chance that you hold this book in your hands, for by grace and grace alone has this work been accomplished, I simply yielded and said, "Yes", when Jesus Christ extended the call. From that point on, my story became His story.

Psalm 92:9 For Behold thine enemies, oh Lord...For behold thine enemies shall perish

Chapter One:

Framed

Mama always forbid tattling, unless of course the matter was a matter of life and death… and so it is!

I need to qualify the fact that before I took my first drink of alcohol at five years of age, I was framed for addiction. Before I told my first lie or even knew what a drug was at ten years of age, I was framed. Before I discovered my counterfeit calling of "Cocaine Cowgirl" transporting untold kilos from South Florida to New York with my former husband, the Colombian I married on my eighteenth birthday...I had been framed. His boss, Pablo Escobar had also been framed.

Maybe you're not guilty of the same type of sins I committed, but according to the Bible, we're all guilty. Romans 3:23 states, (ALL have sinned and fallen short of the glory of God.) Until that fact is well established and settled in our hearts, we don't stand a chance in life or in the afterlife which is guaranteed to be a lot longer!

Personally. I agreed with God on the issue of sin. That's the whole reason I came to Christ in the first place, but because of my gross lack of spiritual knowledge, Satan took full advantage and nominated me, (without my permission, mind you,) as a perfect candidate for destruction.

Unbeknownst to me, I'd also been framed and sealed at salvation by a Power MUCH greater than the tormenting accuser attempting to counterfeit my identity.

I suppose the true motivation behind my urgency in delivering this message is, that had I known earlier what I know now about this spiritual war, perhaps I wouldn't have made such destructive choices throughout my life. If I'd been forewarned of the suggestive power behind my daily confusion and hopelessness, I may have averted the cartel chaos I so willingly embraced as "normal.".

I suspect that because of my familiarity with this chaos, God has called me to warn you, that you too may be the enemy's prey. It doesn't matter who or what led you down your twisted road, the good news is that if you are indeed saved, having acknowledged Jesus Christ as your personal Savior, you are already on the winning side of this battle simply because of who He is and what He accomplished at Calvary.

For many years, Father's eyes gazed longingly into the dark cavern of my stubborn soul, longing for me to finally admit defeat. The counterfeit barriers I'd erected, attempting to shelter me from life's frightening reality, would remain firmly fixed in place until circumstances necessitated a drastic change.

To be honest, it was downright embarrassing to admit that I had totally misjudged God's awesome character. Who could've imagined that the Son of God would wait patiently for those hostile circumstances to force me into a concrete realization of His love?

The gift of forgiveness has so impacted my life, that I wish to extend the same liberty to prisoners currently chained to the demonic infrastructure of sin. The enemy's strategies exist only to garnish our souls with hopelessness, to convince us that there's no way out of our particular circumstance, to assure us that God won't forgive us for the awful things we've done, and to make us question whether we were even saved to begin with.

Having unwittingly allowed the voice of this enemy to become an active part of my daily decisions for so many years qualifies me to testify with utmost accuracy to his deceptive intent and character.
This is that testimony!

Although my discipleship began at the age of eleven, many years would pass before I'd arrive at the profound realization that my life had already been transformed, and hidden in Christ the moment I became born again. (Colossians 3:3)

A broken heart, multiple addictions, unresolved childhood trauma and living on the edge would finally equip my soul with a mysterious willingness to finally discover this spiritual life in Christ that had been sovereignly tucked away. Unbeknownst to me, throughout my years of progressive defeat, God was inconspicuously working behind the scenes, assembling a firm foundation, not only for my benefit but paving the way, that those suffering from the same spiritual blindness might also benefit.

Little did I know that the savage bumps comprising my near-fatal journey, would one day serve to educate a multitude of equally dazed and confused souls. Destined to be fatherless, before the age of two, certainly contributed to my wayward nature, but the majority of my rebellion came simply from my selfish human nature, of which all of us are born equally imprisoned.

For years, I toiled along life's crowded highway, certain that I walked alone; denying my inherent birthright. oblivious to the presence of divine footprints trudging alongside me.

Eventually, I would be instructed by the Holy Spirit exactly how to reclaim my spiritual birthright and I can assure you that it's a treasure I'll never again compromise. Like me, if you trust God with your most painful areas; in time, you'll look back to that very place where the thief stole your most valuable possessions and discover spiritual riches beyond belief.

Those newfound treasures will be so magnificent that, like me, you'll be compelled to share them with the world, proudly placing the contents in a frame for all the world to see.

This is my frame!

  Romans 8:28 NKJV
And we know that all things work together for good to those who love God, to those who are called according to His purpose.

Philippians 1:12
But I want you to know, brethren that the things which happened to me have actually turned out for the furtherance of the gospel.

Chapter Two:

My brother's keeper

Although it has taken many years to properly identify and demolish the walls imprisoning my soul, it did happen and I am one of the Christians who survived the horror to tell the story. You know...the one everybody sings about in church," This is my story, this is my song,"

Deep within my spirit exists tremendous unrest knowing just how many of us haven't made it back home alive, souls prematurely aborted because of this unseen adversary.

Throughout the halls of my memory resides a permanent picture of the hostile demonic guards standing at destiny's door, prohibiting God's unsuspecting children from taking a single step in the direction of freedom.

It grips my heart to reflect upon the unnecessary consequences resulting from my own personal lack of knowledge, the enormous amount of time I wasted participating in and enabling the theft of my legal spiritual inheritance.

Reflecting upon the innocent faces of friends who, for various reasons didn't make it out alive, has birthed within me a violent passion to co-labor with Christ for the plundering of those of us already redeemed by His blood. Someone needs to show them exactly who and what stands in the way of their coveted freedom. There are understandably few Christians who've ventured into the house of captivity to the degree I have, and lived to tell the story. Buckle up buttercup!

If Jesus himself left a flock of 99 to retrieve one lost sheep, who am I to do any less? Seeking to win the lost, while ignoring the found is futile.

The ten years I spent as a prisoner of war, suffering from near spiritual starvation, I'm relieved to know, was simply preparation for a later chapter in my life. This one!

I was certain that because of my behavior or lack of "works" God had given up on me, when the fact of the matter is, I became a Christian ETERNALLY and UNCONDITIONALLY, the moment I believed.

There is no sliding scale Christianity as I'd heard preached, nor does "works" affect our salvation positively or negatively in ANY way. Salvation is a FREE gift… (emphasis on FREE) ... a gift never retracted, a Covenant between the Father and the Son, guaranteeing that not a single one of us will be lost.
Whew! Very Good News for those of us who've slipped up in the" works" department!

Having unnecessarily resided in that house of suffering for so many years, I've chosen to walk back in time to reexamine and endorse the eternal security of the believer, a jarred door of misunderstanding so prevalent in our churches today. Those willing to grasp its relevance with sincere hearts, God has promised, will possess hope and security beyond measure.

***The millisecond a person accepts the gospel, we pass from the kingdom of darkness into the kingdom of light, presenting a potential and substantial threat to the powers of darkness. Armed with limited knowledge of spiritual warfare, new Christians instantaneously become pawns in the hand of an enemy we've denied the existence of. Soon after conversion, we sign an unconscious contract with our Savior's defeated foe, likened to spiritual amnesia, be it addiction, depression, fill in the blank, subconsciously binding our fragile wills to the enemy's destructive agenda.

Believing we have no other choice than to remain in the self-imposed fortress of destruction, we anesthetize ourselves to the best of our ability, ever conscious of the debilitating effects of sin, yet fully embracing the lie that we're powerless to do anything about it. We take the enemy's bait without even a willingness to question its relevance to our destiny.

The adversary's demons stand guard at the entrance of our wayward souls, laughing at our despair, forbidding our escape, obtaining orders to carry out the necessary orders to prevent our release.

Voices of accusation daily haunt us, reminding us of what we've always erroneously believed, that deep down, we're hopeless and helpless, ill-equipped to function in this world. Although we may be visibly absent from a church's congregation, we KNOW that the holy incorruptible seed was indeed eternally implanted upon conversion. Only a few of us care enough to seek the truth in spite of the lie and most often because of the lie., The Truth beckons each of us to take a deeper look, but tragically because of the lie, few ever will. Only by accepting the Truth will any of us perceive the lie, renounce it and fulfill our earthly destinies.

The erroneous doctrine that believers are capable of losing salvation is one that blatantly denies the Holy Spirit's ability to work beyond the four walls of "organized" religion. endorsing the ridiculous lie that the "Counselor" is somehow less capable of counseling His own beyond the man-made structure of a building.

God is faithful to complete the work that He alone initiated in the lives of each His children, regardless of their present-day location, and doesn't depend upon our skill set or lack thereof to complete that task. A person born of the Spirit of God, like it or not, is eternally secure and unconditionally bound for glory.

The true status of an heir will NEVER be contingent upon our meager contribution to the family, regardless of how good or talented we think we are, simply because none of us had anything of value to contribute in the first place.

Unfortunately, some of us experience the deadly grip of sin's power before awakening to the blessed revelation that Jesus Christ completely destroyed that power. Just as Christians do nothing to inherit eternal life by becoming born again, we do nothing at all to receive the awful sinful nature of which we all share, apart from being born into this corrupt and fallen world.

Tragically, when trusted leaders within the body of Christ ascertain that prodigals have lost their salvation because of fleshly behavior, it drives us to that exact destination... Destruction! Cornering the prodigal against the seemingly impenetrable wall of deception is Satan himself, convincing many of God's children that if God is against them, (as evidenced by their difficult circumstances,) why not give up the fight altogether?

There, in that perilous corner of defeat, we subconsciously ignore the inner prompting to challenge this invisible enemy, simply because we've yet to discern that there is indeed an enemy standing in the way.

We will be shocked to see the number of saints who died having yielded to an enemy they knew nothing about, but because of Christ's righteousness, were no less worthy than saints having spent a lifetime inside the institutional church setting.

On that day, Christian leaders will be grieved to realize how many earthly lives were aborted or lost because they refused to preach the liberating gospel of salvation through faith in Christ alone.

Forfeiting the weapons of their warfare, these fragile souls lived their lives naked and ashamed, as the host of hell stood mocking the remarkable ignorance employed by another child of God.

According to a 2020 Barna survey, only 51% of Americans believe in a traditional, biblical view of God as the all-powerful, all knowing, perfect and just Creator. Of those who said they believe, more people said that Jesus "sinned," than didn't (44-41%) and an even higher percentage believe in Satan (56%) than believe in God. Something fatally wrong with these statistics, my friend!

Having yet been versed on how to challenge these lies, Christians sink down as far as we're willing to be pushed. Unfortunately, for some, it's to an early grave. Don't let that someone be you! Arm yourself and see how dangerous YOU really are!

~Behold thine enemy and allow the Truth to set you free! Ignore the Truth and remain a prisoner eternally. ~

"And this is the Father's will which hath sent me, that of ALL which he hath given me I should lose nothing, but should raise it up again at the last day." (John 6:39;)

Chapter Three:
Orphans in the storm

While the world understands an orphan to be an individual with no parents, I use the term "spiritual orphan" to describe a person who lacks a spiritual Father, which is a commonality that we all share at birth: a separation from God the Father.

I was born, as we all are, a spiritual orphan and at 18 months old was destined to become physically fatherless due to the death of my father in a car accident. I then prayed to God, as a child, not for dolls or games, but simply for a daddy, only to discover, as many of us do, that not all daddies are good.

I collected memories of abuse and neglect far into adulthood with scrapbook after scrapbook of lingering memories that refused to loosen their deadly grip on an already uncertain destiny. Concealing secrets of sexual, physical and emotional abuse, I internalized the resulting shame, entitlement and rebellion embracing them as daily companions. Perceived or real rejection propelled me to repress emotions and shrink back from anything or anyone healthy, internalizing a sense of abandonment, loneliness, alienation and isolation, not only from the outside world, but ultimately a total rejection of myself.

If we have no connection to our earthly father or an unhealthy connection at best, our identity is at increased risk of developing a counterfeit identity.

Betrayal, abandonment and suspicion linger long after the abuse occurs, following us, like childhood companions we've readily accepted as friends, yet the majority of us never even question their relevance in our lives, having no idea that these daily companions of guilt and shame are simply and profoundly the resulting consequences of unresolved childhood trauma.

An orphan, (spiritual or physical) struggles with self-worth, overcompensating with performance orientation, constantly striving to achieve gratification, through using people and loving things, instead of loving people and using things. struggling to gain satisfaction through the use of various substances or people in their lives, striving for success through material possessions, work, drugs, alcohol, relationships... anything to fill up the gaping hole in our hearts.

These vulnerable souls with extraordinary self-esteem issues are a perfect target for the enemy, gravitating, ever so innocently into the occult, prostitution, drugs & alcohol, anywhere in a frenzied attempt to" find themselves." Denied genuine protection and provision in life and lacking intimate relationships to model after, we truly believe we have no intrinsic value and must" perform" to please.

When one is abandoned or rejected by their earthly father, a deep void is created, making it impossible for a healthy interaction with our heavenly Father, even as a Christian. Studies indicate that one in four children grow up in homes without a father and that those of us lacking a relationship with our genetic fathers often develop identity problems, thus becoming a perfect target for a counterfeit identity. According to the statistics, we're not supposed to make it; and only those of us choosing to recognize the significance of our spiritual inheritance and fight for it +will make it!

When our eyes have finally been opened to the reality of this war, no power in hell dare cross over the bloodline to reach us, because we KNOW IN WHOM WE BELIEVE.

Once upon a time, I listened to no one and resented everyone, until my life depended upon believing someone. *That" Someone" is now my everything.*

By His grace I have entered the good land which the Lord our God has promised as an inheritance. I have victoriously crossed over, despite forgetting His covenant of protection to me, a fatherless child. Because of that grace, my days have been prolonged, and by that same grace I will serve Him for as long as He gives me physical breath.

As runaways and prodigals, we lose so many people and possessions in life and we truly believe that" salvation" was on that list. I'm blessed to have finally discovered that what was spiritually" found" can never be lost, what was born-again, can never be aborted, for my salvation was solely and irretrievably purchased by Jesus Christ. I am no longer an orphan!

My mission is now to convince YOU of that fact.

Is it possible to accept a counterfeit identity as a Christian?
Can a" true" Christian be" lost?"
Is eternal security truly" secure"?
Follow me and see for yourself that" not all who wander are lost."

Jesus said, "I will not leave you as orphans," (John 14:18)

"In love, he predestined us to be adopted as his sons through Jesus Christ, in accordance with his pleasure and will." — Ephesians 1:5

FYI..

If you're NOT yet a Christian, you remain DIRECTLY under the influence of Satan whether you choose to believe that or not.

Run......don't walk to Jesus Christ while time permits. I promise you'll be eternally grateful you did.

Salvation...is simple as the ABC's Don't let ANYONE convince you otherwise!

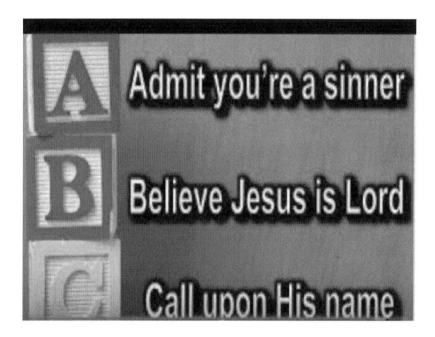

Chapter Four:
Born again at eleven

In the presence of our enemy, we passed from spiritual death to spiritual life; instantly and eternally born into the glorious kingdom of God. I was eleven, and my best friend was ten. Neither of us had any idea that a war even existed for heaven's sake, let alone imagine we were being framed and that our lives would be targeted for destruction beyond our wildest dreams.

For years we lived and moved and had our beings in the presence of the Savior…while this unseen enemy feverishly calculated our end. Eventually Suzie and I went different directions in life; both still blatantly unaware of our great spiritual heritage, having no idea of the God given inheritance Satan sought so desperately to conceal.

For years I allowed my sin nature to pummel me harshly to the ground below, determined each time to get back up to fight with an enemy whose existence I had yet to understand, unarmed on life's bloody battlefield, watching my life steadily worsen with each blow.

Being the obstinate one that I am, I had to come crashing hard to that ground below before finally recognizing the need for divine intervention.

And to the sheer delight of that unseen enemy; two thousand miles away, my best friend also came violently crashing to the ground. The difference in our falls was that at the tender age of twenty-three, she wouldn't have the opportunity to get back up; her physical life was brutally and senselessly aborted at the hands of a cruel assassin who came only to steal, kill and destroy.

-It is in her honor and memory that this book is dedicated. -

Finishing her sentence:

I've often wondered exactly what Suzie would say to the world if she still had the opportunity. I know she'd long for you to know the truth about your salvation and the inheritance that accompanies it; and because I knew that girl like a book, I'm sure she'd be delighted to expose Satan's schemes in hopes that even one of you might escape and survive.

As little girls I had a fascinating way of finishing her sentences...simply because she stuttered and I had little patience. If only she understood back then that Jesus Christ finished her death sentence once and for all, she might still be here today to testify to His amazing grace. But she's not. She's with our Savior; not because of what she did or didn't do here on earth but because of His faithfulness to His own promise. If only we'd understood the price He paid on our behalf or the distance He traveled to fulfill that sacrifice.

I imagine the joy she must've felt the moment she gazed into His face. I'm certain she felt relieved, because like me, she blindly allowed the enemy to lead her so far down the road to destruction that she actually believed there wasn't any hope for someone like her. Like me, she'd allowed the enemy to accompany her to the edge of a night so brutal and dark that it makes me shudder to even think about it. Unlike me, she's no longer alive to share the details of that fatal night.

We were both orphans in the storm, denied the inherent privilege of knowing and loving an earthly father; mine because of death, hers, just plain absent. Although we were sincere when we gave our hearts to Christ at that tender age, we hadn't a clue how to relate to a loving heavenly Father, and that vital lack of knowledge became the enemy's prime opportunity to counterfeit and destroy.

When I gaze back in time, I see two innocent children, who, because of troubling and even demonic circumstances in life, were clearly framed. I see two unsuspecting victims set up for failure because they neglected to embrace that the Gospel, they'd received at that young age was eternal, not based on works, never to be lost and as I look around at the multitudes around me in life, I can't help but wonder how many of us share that same frightening statistic. How many of us still wander a crooked path, thinking God is mad simply because they've yet to embrace the true gospel…that Jesus Christ is COMMITTED to never leaving or forsaking them?

Although I can't retrieve yesterday, perhaps God will help me to reach even one of the orphans still missing that they, too, might live and not die.
After all,.... all's fair in love and war, and it has become my personal mission to give the devil his due!
Exposure!

I often wonder exactly how my friend's destiny might have played out here on earth, had she not forfeited her birthright. Perhaps I won't know those answers until I get to glory, but I'm confident that Suzie wouldn't mind one bit if I took the liberty to finish her sentence just one more time.

Being the louder and bolder of the two, I never gave a hoot what people thought about my words nor did I care about the penalty of their sting, until I dealt with resulting consequences. I'm still just as loud and bold as I was back then; only now I speak with a different authority, a different passion and I absolutely DO care what you think about my words, because if you just so happen to be an orphan or prodigal wandering out in that wilderness trying to "rough" it all alone, you're destined to become a casualty just like her.

And you never know, finishing her sentence MAY just prevent that tragedy from occurring. Keeping you in the dark is precisely the enemy's strategy; unless you position yourself to receive nothing less than the spiritual birthright Jesus Christ died to bestow upon you.

I'm grateful that the crown isn't given to the swiftest or the wisest but simply to he who finishes the race. The details of my journey will probably be insignificant to you if you're not a prodigal but if you are, we were destined to meet long before I drew my first breath.

Father saw each of us from afar. He knew each of our names and exactly what our journey in life would comprise. He also knew which of us would become prodigals and why….and which of us would become casualties….and when. And those of us who survived, He would call to be eyewitnesses. I am one of those witnesses that got away…...for such a time as this.

~ My words won't bring Suzi back nor can they erase the damage Satan caused but I pray that my testimony reaches YOU. That would be justice enough for Me!~

He was a murderer from the beginning, and does not stand in the truth, because there is no truth in him. When he speaks a lie, he speaks from his own resources, for he is a liar and the father of it.   John 8:44b NKJV

Chapter Five:

Rules of engagement

 Imagine being seductively led into enemy territory without a bit of ammunition, and suddenly realizing that your destination isn't at all" friendly" territory; but in fact, quite the opposite. You've been led so far into the enemy's domain that you've actually forgotten what road you took to get there, and have no idea how to turn around.

 Terrified, you discover that every road you embark upon is a dead end. You've completely lost your way, and the only" friends" you've come to know are the enemy's friends and you clearly can't trust" his" friends.

A faint voice deep down within has given you THAT much information about this war.

That" SOMEONE" is the Holy Spirit, my friend, the Victor who accompanies us as we blindly waltz into enemy territory, the same "SOMEONE" who continues to clothe us in our nakedness, defeating great armies before us without our knowledge.

He instructed us on this" battle" in the bible, effectively preparing us for warfare. In fact, the entire Word of God addresses this war, but because I was utterly convinced that God was furious with me, His word was the LAST place I would've looked for relief. While I was rapidly perishing in battle, that same" SOMEONE", that I'd called upon at the altar at eleven years of age was fulfilling every word of His promise.

Although I've never been a soldier in a physical war, from what I've been told, a whole lot of preparation goes into training for the battlefield.

Years of grueling maneuvers instructing soldiers on how to escape and survive a possible ambush are rehearsed, day in and day out preparing them for what could be...should it ever be.

It is to that soldier's best interest to learn basic skills for his survival; learning how to properly utilize his weapons and most importantly: understanding exactly who his enemy is and if he's even on the correct side of the battlefield.

Not only is it in that soldier's best interest to pay attention and receive appropriate instruction, it is also the responsibility of the government to provide such training.

One of the devil's tactics is to perpetually pull the veil of darkness over his character and domain so the world won't understand who he is. The devil knows—as do military leaders in any battle -- that we must understand the enemy or we simply won't be prepared to even fight, let alone defeat him.

God the Father has taken every possible measure to equip His children for this battle, guaranteeing a certain and lasting victory. Having previously missed the mark, I'm grateful that my captivity will now serve to educate, illustrate and prayerfully provide a way of escape for those remaining on the wrong side of this bloody battlefield.

Your deliverance from the enemy's camp will depend upon believing and receiving the Truth of God's Word. Nothing more...nothing less...and your biggest obstacle isn't convincing yourself that God WILL deliver you…it's understanding and appropriating the fact that HE ALREADY HAS.

This information might sound too simplistic, but the first step in dealing with spiritual warfare is to simply recognize that you're in a war! This is half the battle!

Remember that the enemy likes to operate in darkness. (Eph 5:8-13), and often, as was in my case, he darkens our understanding of true grace!

Depending upon what you've been taught, it might surprise you to know that maintaining your salvation wasn't up to you in the first place! Simply acknowledging your need for salvation and accepting Jesus Christ's atoning sacrifice on your behalf was all it took to become ETERNALLY His.

We didn't earn His acceptance; and neither can we lose it, despite harmful opinions and toxic doctrine to the contrary. We are saved by grace alone; through faith alone, in Christ alone… not of works lest any man should boast, but because of lack of knowledge and improper training, many of us needlessly remain missing in action, most typically sitting in the enemy's camp, pretending to have a" good time."

My deliverance out of enemy territory had nothing to do with me and everything to do with the wonderful Commanding Officer I had accused of abandoning me.

Religious scoffers, of course ascertain that prodigals aren't Christians at all; blah, blah, blah, but God is not a man that He should lie and His own Word promises eternal security. Someone else is lying my friend and you can bet that your enemy is the twisted author of that lie and the primary reason so many remain M.I.A.

After becoming born again at salvation, the catastrophe is that some of us aren't warned of the bad news; that we have just become a walking target to Satan, the roaring lion, seeking whom he may devour.

Without complete understanding of the Good News, some of us are placed in a more precarious position than we began. Denial or ignorance of the enemy's existence doesn't make him any less of a threat, but in fact more. If I jump off of a building, I'll plunge to my death, just like anyone else because I've chosen not to believe in the physical law of gravity; likewise, with spiritual laws!!

Jesus Christ will always mediate our case, despite what our denominations, parents or authorities have taught us, in spite of what our emotions feel, simply because Jesus Christ is faithful to His own.

Thank God that our release from captivity is, was and will forever be fully dependent upon grace; never secured by our own human effort. We may" feel" like we have no rights, our mind may" trick" us into believing that freedom is impossible, irrational and undeserved; emotions may scream daily, reminding us of failure, prompting us to "repay" graces bestowed upon us, BUT our Divine Mediator said, "It is finished! We are free…pardoned eternally and payback…totally inconceivable.

Counterfeit ID (Internal dialogue)

Not only are Christians oblivious that God speaks to our spirits, we remain hopelessly ignorant of the fact that Satan speaks to our souls, (mind, will and emotions,) whispering his counterfeit agenda, facilitating the fable that we have no real purpose in life, the annoying voice of accusation begging us to end it all.

Of course, back then, I wouldn't have believed the far-fetched explanation about a spiritual war simply because I was convinced that I knew it all.

Why would Satan want to counterfeit MY identity?

Why would he be so interested in terminating MY life and what could he possibly gain from My death? It might surprise you. It did me.

It's taken me decades to understand the true dynamics of this war, but now that I've been enlightened, I couldn't be convinced otherwise. Satan understands that once this vital spiritual information leaks out; once a believer understands their TRUE identity in this war, nothing shall be impossible.

When I grasped the magnitude of how many prodigals really do exist, God birthed in me a fierce determination to cross enemy lines, one more time...this time, armed and dangerous.

You betcha my zeal has been met with incredible resistance from the opposing side, but considering that the war was already won, what have I got to lose?

Just for the record, had I died in my blatant sin, God's grace would've been standing there with arms open wide, waiting to receive me, just like He was for Suzi; heartbroken that my lack of knowledge generated the premature death of my physical body, disappointed because I allowed myself to be robbed of the earthly identity prepared for me.

Like it or not, when we accept Jesus Christ as our personal Savior, we actively enlist in a spiritual war. At that moment recorded in all of eternity, we turned in our earthly grave clothes to our unseen Commanding Officer; Jesus Christ and exchanged them for His heavenly battle attire.

An invisible spiritual exchange took place at that moment in time, so invisible that most of us dismissed the significance, remaining needless prisoners of war, lying helplessly, smack dab in enemy territory, in the same grave clothes of addiction, clinging to the identical rags we handed into our Commanding Officer upon conversion.

Of course, the enemy wanted me to die in the valley of the shadow of my addiction specifically that I couldn't see what I see now. I suppose he took great delight in imprisoning me for so many years, unlawfully holding my body and soul captive, torturing my mind unnecessarily, while I clung tightly to those counterfeit grave clothes.

I suppose he thought it quite amusing watching this child of God squirm and panic as my life took a deeper, darker turn, seemingly without a way out. I suppose also that as he walked back and forth policing my mind with his lies, he had absolutely no idea about the book you now hold in your hands.

I doubt he had any idea whatsoever that I was taking notes during my stay in his kingdom, notes that would one day become public knowledge, notes that would one day turn a multitude back to Jesus Christ.

For a long time, I was just so grateful to be out of enemy territory, that I neglected to give it much thought, until the day My Commanding Officer approached me about publishing the notes I had written as a prisoner in this spiritual war, notes that might help you to glance down at your own ID (internal dialogue) and suspect that you, too just might be a victim of identity fraud.

Because God isn't a respecter of persons, I'm convinced that what He's done for me, He'll do for you, if you simply acknowledge His miraculous ability to do so.

If you're a true prodigal, you've already sensed deep down inside that something is desperately wrong, (compliments of the residing Holy Spirit) but because of lack of knowledge, remain incapable of defining this war...

Because a prodigal no longer fits into traditional society, he's daily subjected to spiritual contradictions beyond his ability to comprehend.

In desperation, his soul seeks out people, substances, possessions, anything to fill that void.

His friends, opportunistically won't be Christians, so how will he know, if someone doesn't' set out to inform him?

Just how in this world, will an uneducated prodigal survive, if someone doesn't seek him out? It's highly unusual for this type to just wake up one day and consciously decide to go to church.

From personal experience, I can testify that prodigals won't possess a natural tenacity to force open a door that's" seemingly" bolted shut by the enemy, especially a church door.

Nevertheless, Jesus Christ faithfully stands knocking on the door they've been tricked into believing is permanently shut. These prodigals need special education, my friend, an education provided not by manuals, lectures or faulty church doctrine!

Reflecting upon the experiences of former prodigals, may enable them to recognize how their OWN life patterns share an uncanny synchronization.

After studying the subject of dependency and childhood sexual abuse for over 30 years, I've concluded that unresolved grief contributes to the majority of dysfunctional behaviors so prevalent amongst us, especially in the church.

None of us are capable of experiencing the thrill of Christ's victory until we've felt the agony of fleshly defeat. Some Christians float about aimlessly in life, truly believing that they're affecting a change for the kingdom of God, when, sadly, they've yet to allow the Holy Spirit to uncork years of their own bottled-up grief.

Until we've struggled against the enemy's hateful grip of fleshly defeat, we've yet to experience the glorious release. sleeping with an enemy we've innocently welcomed as a friend. Despair not, though, dear believer, for this cause the Son of God was manifest....to destroy the works of the devil.

1 John 3:8

May the same God who breathed the words, "let there be light," flood your entire being with the spiritual revelation necessary, equipping you with the wisdom necessary to enlighten and sustain your soul. A simple, "I surrender, Lord", will suffice.

I can attest firsthand that the enemy will fight against you stronger than ever, but having established a newfound trust in your Savior's sufficiency is all the ammunition you'll ever need.

Many false teachers and religions attempt to convince Christians that we need to add to the crucifixion and resurrection but Jesus Christ gave us the GIFT of eternal life, independent of works, the moment we received Him...FOREVER!

He birthed us into the Kingdom the moment we said, "I do." Therefore, hold fast to that truth regardless of the depths to which you've fallen because if anyone believes that the completed work at Calvary can be lost or retracted for any reason whatever, Jesus Christ has died in vain. For by grace, you have been saved through faith, and that not of yourselves; it is the gift of God, not of works, lest anyone should boast. Ephesians 2:8-9

The ten years I spent as a prisoner of war, suffering from near spiritual starvation, I'm relieved to know, was simply preparation for a later chapter in my life. This one.!

My release from captivity represents more now, than my own personal freedom, it represents justice and liberty for you! When I asked God why He has entrusted ME with the undeniable privilege of broadcasting these truths…I could almost hear Him chuckle," Because it takes one to know one." Rock bottom simply became a launching pad to complete His call!

Are you ready to fight for what is yours, or does passivity suit you?

If the latter be the case, understand that God's Spirit will not strive with willful compromise. That doesn't mean that salvation is lost. Salvation is totally independent of works, but the resulting consequences of passivity will sadly be a definitive loss of reward and miserable life here upon earth.

Denying the inheritance that our Savior scorned His own shame to purchase, many of us will incur the greater loss. If we're going to fight for something valuable, why not fight for a sure thing...a promise faithfully written down in both stone and blood.

FYI. Remember, if you are not "born again" you have absolutely no power over your flesh. You may believe you do, but your flesh as well as mine was born into the virtual condition of sin, and the only antidote for that diseased condition is the blood of Jesus Christ.

Simply admit your sinful condition, believe that Jesus Christ died in your place to deliver you eternally from the power of sin and death and embrace the glorious gospel of your salvation. It's not a formal thing at all. It doesn't even need to be performed in a church building. Having accepted Christ's atoning sacrifice on our behalf, we have BECOME the literal church! Doesn't get much better than THAT friend!

For by grace, you have been saved through faith, and that not of yourselves; it is the GIFT OF GOD, not of works, lest anyone should boast. Ephesians 2:8-9

1 Corinthians 15:1-4 KJV

Moreover, brethren, I declare unto you the gospel which I preached unto you, which also ye have received, and wherein ye stand; By which also ye are saved, if ye keep in memory what I preached unto you, unless ye have believed in vain. For I delivered unto you first of all that which I also received, how that Christ died for our sins according to the scriptures; And that he was buried, and that he rose again the third day according to the scriptures.

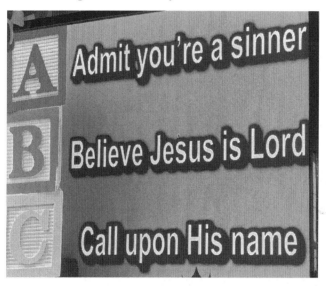

If YOU just so happen to be a fallen soldier, you can take this information or leave it; but rest assured if you choose the latter, you may just reach the Promised Land sooner than you expected without ever having comprehended

that you were on the winning side of this spiritual battle all along. Soldier, know your rights!"
~Bottom line...We are engaged in a spiritual war that Jesus Christ already won.

2 Timothy 2:4 No soldier in active service entangles himself in the affairs of everyday life, so that he may please the one who enlisted him as a soldier.

1Peter 5:8 Be self-controlled and alert. Your enemy the devil prowls around like a roaring lion looking for someone to devour.
The devil is the "prince of the power of the air." (Eph. 2:2) operates in the atmosphere around us, and without spiritual ammunition to fight this new found adversary, new believers, ignorant of his devices, are his most vulnerable prey..~ .
The sacrifices of God are a broken spirit, A broken and a contrite heart-- These, O God, You will not despise. Psalms 51:1

Chapter Six: Web of lies

O, what a tangled web we weave when first we practice to deceive! Walter Scott

When life forces us to see the cruelty of this world at a very early age…. we're literally" trapped." Like a spider weaving its delicate web, are the lies indoctrinated into our souls from well-meaning parents, religious organizations and other significant authority figures who honestly believe" they're "instructing" and "educating."

This invisible web can and does often begin before birth, entangling its twisted roots deeply into our personalities, cleverly extending a counterfeit identity with the sole purpose of assassinating the TRUE character that we were spiritually destined to receive.

My web

Not only was my perception of God and religion totally misleading," someone" had to convince me that my identity was other than what the Word of God stated it was.

Someone had to whisper subtle lies that I believed and received as truth.

Having been inducted into Catholicism at an early age, I perceived God to be a punishing, unreachable deity who would remain displeased with my behavior regardless of how hard I tried. Although that is partly correct, (all have sinned and fallen short of the glory of God- Romans 3:23)., that religion failed to inform me that Jesus Christ became my propitiation (substitute) granting me complete peace with God...peace based SOLELY upon the fulfillment of HIS death and resurrection, never based upon my works or lack of works, or failing to perform forbidden practices such as praying to Mary or departed saints.

Contrary to popular opinion, like that spider web, the human soul remains distorted in its thinking, perceptions, and conclusions until we become born again and allow the Holy Spirit of God the opportunity to unravel and transform our faulty perceptions. Weaved into our subconscious minds, the traps and snares of the enemy blind us, like cobwebs in our minds, they lay hidden and out of sight distorting our perceptions and blocking out light.

For me, the idea of anything or anyone in authority even remotely close to me made me shudder, for the simple reason that my trust had been violated through sexual abuse ae a young child. That victimization served as cement in the foundation of my soul, crippling my ability to trust, programming me to rebel, run and hide from anyone in authority, including and most especially God.

I internalized the lie that I had to perform to be accepted and because of my gross inability to perform anything acceptable to God, why even try?

Little did I know that God had already ETERNALLY bridged the gap between my ungodliness and His holiness the nanosecond I believed the gospel message at eleven years of age and received Jesus Christ as my personal Savior. I had absolutely no idea that His power could and would transform my scarred soul with its many strongholds, nor was I yet aware that such strongholds even existed.

Due to this ignorance of spiritual warfare; and the enemy's relentless pursuit, it would take years until I'd finally hearken to the glorious voice of my Savior. Only then, would the Holy Spirit commence to unravel the complexity of my" web," and release me from the demonic cement encasing my soul.

Often, as was in my case, the entanglement begins before birth. A prime example; my mother casually visited a fortune teller when she was pregnant with me, and that demonic agent, without hesitation, told her that she was carrying a boy; a lie that my mother wholeheartedly believed and received without understanding that this modest act of curiosity opened wide a portal to the demonic realm.

Although she was surprised and even blessed that the baby, she had been carrying was a girl... that seemingly" innocent" betrayal was the first opportunistic foothold that the spirit of rejection would initiate in the life of my soul.

Adding fuel to the fire, my dad was killed when I was 18 months old, reinforcing that stronghold of rejection, establishing a vacancy that none but a fatherless child would understand. This vacancy provided the perfect breeding ground for the enemy to offer toxic alternatives to a heart desperately seeking to" escape," and I can assure you that I latched on to the bait without resistance.

I can't educate you on how the deceptive web of lies began in your life, I can only testify why a false identity formed on my behalf and how this unseen enemy played a pivotal part.

At five years of age I was sexually abused, and threatened that if I ever told anyone, both myself and my mother would be murdered. Who, but a hostile enemy would viciously clothe a child with such shame and crippling fear?

My soul internalized that shame and because of another man's sin, I BECAME a shame-based person, totally silencing the budding character yet to form. Because these destructive events were never addressed, my self-image quickly evolved into a classic rebel with a rapidly developing alcohol and drug addiction, ever so desperately seeking to anesthetize the pain that so desperately sought to consume me.

As a teenager, I began to steal on a regular basis after my Papa's death from cancer, cars, retail, whatever I wanted, justifying in my twisted mind the attitude that I" deserved" it," life was unfair," and that God must be mad at me to take both my father and the man who raised me.

Today I know that I stole back then because my innocence was stolen from me...simple as that; my entire childhood, with any hopes and dreams of a future were viciously and senselessly aborted by the hand of my perpetrator and I simply lacked the resources to further heal.

So indeed, the enemy gains a substantial foothold in childhood due to demonic environmental activity; a variable we had absolutely no control over. Looking back, I don't recall that I was ever intentionally fascinated or willingly approved of evil in my life; fearful, maybe, but never "fascinated".

I never consciously provoked its visitation into my life, I can assure you of that, but neither did I have the power to prevent its crippling effects. The atmosphere I grew up in as a child played a key role in contributing to the daily sense of impending doom I experienced, programming my heart to expect the worst. It was a perfect storm, a set up for enemy seduction.

Domestic, physical and sexual abuse in any home provides a platform for victimization, often taking years to discover that these early childhood experiences are the actual roots to our foundational strongholds. Going forward, I would then experience life in a state of betrayal trauma as an angry, unsuspecting victim without a clue.

At seventeen I ran away from home (Western Pa.) to Miami Beach where I would meet and marry, on my eighteenth birthday, one of Pablo Escobar's prime cartel runners, only to develop a cocaine addiction exceeding $1,000 a day of which I wouldn't pay a dime. Tell me THAT wasn't a stroke of luck. (Slick devil!)
 ***Stay tuned for that next book, ("Cocaine Cowgirl," currently underway.)

That same year, (1979...during the Iranian hostage crisis), through no fault of my own I was struck by a speeding car in Miami Beach (coincidentally by an Iranian behind the wheel of an Avis rental) while crossing a major highway .... broke the windshield with my face, (mom always said I had a hard head;) also broke tibia, fibula and femur in my left leg, hospitalizing me for months with Dr. 's guaranteeing that I'd never walk again. Thankfully they were wrong! I could go on and on with the well-crafted sophistication of my web but this isn't about me anymore, it's about you. If you let Jesus Christ disclose and unravel the lies the enemy spoon fed you, He will!

God was there when the web was spun and He desperately desires to uncover damaging secrets you've yet to even discover about yourself while there is yet time. ONLY He can prevent spiritual cobwebs from becoming what we so deceptively embrace as earthly decorations we so readily embrace as character flaws.

Today, I see the enemy's web corrupting the world we live in, but am not touched by it, I can look at it straight in the face and never be threatened or immobilized by fear, for greater is the power that worketh in me, than the cowardly power that challenged me. In my desperation, I have cautiously learned to abandon myself to God, relinquishing toxic emotions, irrational conclusions and the required faith that ferociously spun that wicked web.

When you know better, you do better. Simple as that!

God didn't chastise me for my faulty belief system, nor did He punish me for repeating defective generational patterns. He just switched on the Light, tore the web down and helped me build a new foundation.
*He IS a carpenter, after all!

Bottom line: Sin is a prison and we're all sentenced to death……
But God!!!

Ephesians 5:13, KJV: "But all things that are reproved are made manifest by the light: for whatsoever doth make manifest is light."

For by grace, you have been saved through faith, and that not of yourselves; it is the GIFT OF GOD, not of works, lest anyone should boast. Ephesians 2:8-9

Part two: Created Crisis

Chapter Seven:
Behind the mask

Who is Satan?

The Prisoner

I know that there's a devil, for his demons had me in chains, a prisoner of sin and torment that started out as an innocent game.

My hands were tied behind me with handcuffs made of steel. This life was one big question mark...my nightmare was very real.

I wanted to run just as fast as I could, to where I did not know, hoping to escape hell's fire and find shelter away from this foe.

Through my journey into darkness. I felt a hand reach out to me, he said that he was my Savior and only His blood could set me free.

He handed me the Book of Life and His words were very clear; "This is My plan for all of mankind...you'll find your way in here."

-Basically, that was my life in a" nutshell," a prisoner. Life was a constant state of confusion, chaos and drama and I truly had no clue why. Like a pawn in the game of life, I was merely along for the ride retaining zero power to change or question my direction. Who knew??? And if someone DID know…why didn't they notify me? Thus...my urgency to actively inform you.

Many people do not know that the devil at one time actually served God, inhabiting Heaven. The prophet Isaiah gives us a glimpse into what caused his fall, resulting in his becoming our adversary. God did not create "Satan;" rather, He created the most glorious angel in Heaven, known as "Lucifer, son of the morning." He was majestically beautiful, but is now sinister with dark supernatural ability operating from high places.

The Bible refers to Satan as the deceiver, destroyed, liar, murder and thief whose sole purpose is to steal, kill and destroy whatever and whomever he can, while he still can.

We all have different images or definitions of what or who an enemy might be. Some say it's the obvious evil existing within our daily world; i.e., thieves, rapists, murderers, Taliban, Isis, KKK, Hitler's unthinkable murder of over six million Jews...or on a more personal level, a deceptive, unfair boss, cheating ex-spouse, you name it, the list goes on and on. He's the influencer of all evil and works through whomever allows him access. When Lucifer fell, He took one-third of the angels with him. We call them demons, and Satan is their master.

Many people imagine the devil to be that little red man in cartoons with horns, tights and a tail holding a pitchfork... ...a dangerous and harmless depiction...ever so far from the truth and exactly what he wants the world to believe.

Match.com's new ad is precisely what I'm talking about. In the video, Satan and 2020 (a female with a dating profile) conveniently hooks up on Match.com. This snippet of," Love Story," by Taylor Swift has been viewed millions of times by an impressionable audience, encouraging a dangerously harmful depiction of "innocence."

    Just like the enemy to put a twist of sick humor and innocence on himself when portraying the harmless character, he wants the world to think he is", as he poses for selfies with his new" match," 2020" in front of the dumpster, even rushing to the" church" to get married...characterizing himself as clever, appealing, appetizing, harmless, and even…. God forbid a" match."
Getting the picture yet?

    Before he fell, "Satan in his original wisdom and beauty was the consummation of perfection." Now his profane hunger is to pull God down from His throne (impossible feat) by endeavoring to distort God's glory in the hearts and minds of those who seek Him.

The Bible also describes Satan as a" light bearer." so we know for certain he must have a beautiful side or at least a deceptively satisfying side or why would Hollywood be so intrigued? Yep, you're catching on...the influence of demonic spirits.

2 Corinthians 4:4 says the devil is called "The god of this world." So, we know demonic forces are certainly at work, influencing world leaders, the fake media, our faulty belief systems and perceptions.

Actually, Satan is the existing force behind every work of darkness, the internal dialogue inside of everyone's head screaming that we're not ok, that we'll never be O.K., that God is mad at us, blah, blah, blah..

Some of his most common titles :Devil (Slanderer) Lucifer (son of the morning,) Prince of darkness, angel of light, god of this world, father of lies, Beelzebub, Belial, roaring lion, serpent, dragon, Accuser. He is the adversary of God and God's lineage and you can bet that as long as he's permitted access, he will relentlessly plot to deceive and distract the world with special" coverage" on the elect.

Have you ever considered just what or who he came to steal, kill and destroy and why? It might be to your advantage to find out because you, my friend, are not exempt from his radar. A true treasure (our spiritual inheritance) can't be stolen, but it can certainly be hidden from our sight.

As evidenced by the media and current headlines; racism, hatred, rioting, looting, vandalism and murder share today's spotlight and you betcha Satan has everything to do with that spotlight.

The devil doesn't just shake your hand and say," pleased to meet you, won't you guess my name." On the contrary, he beguiles us into believing that we're receiving extraordinary privileges or rewards when he offers us his will, ideas, and evil intentions, but sadly that exchange eventually leads only to his ultimate goal of destruction and death.

Since the fall of man in the Garden of Eden, his intent is to deceive the world however he can, by whatever means he can, for as long as he can. The enemy works through whomever allows him access. He is a created spirit being of the order of angels called, "Cherubim" and has a well-structured rank of demons (fallen angels) tending to his business. It's not the Republicans, Democrats or Independents causing this havoc. It's Satan!

1John 3:9 For this reason the Son of God was manifest….to destroy the works of the devil.

And yes, my friend, the works of the devil are more than abortion, death, thievery and destruction, more often they're subtle hidden snares (webs) lying deep within the subconscious mind that, left unresolved eventually lead us down roads God never intended for us to walk, with strangers He never intended for us to meet. Satan will one day be eternally assigned his place in the lake of fire (Revelation 20:15), but now the Bible warns us to," stay alert and watch out for your great enemy, the devil prowls around like a roaring lion, looking for someone to devour." 1Peter5:8 Bottom line.....Don't let that someone be you!

Chapter Eight:

Paranormal Activity... Occult

Satan knows how curious we all are about the future we all are, so he equips fortune-tellers, mediums, palm readers and psychics with familiar spirits to bait the hungry enquirers and nudge them ever so deceptively into the demonic realm.

Although these paranormal avenues may seem fascinating and appealing to the flesh, God forbids any interaction whatsoever with the devil for our own protection as he masquerades as an angel of light (2 Corinthians 11:14.) A recent Gallup survey shows that three in four Americans hold some paranormal belief. Ever wonder why such an interest in the paranormal and metaphysical realm?

Occult books and resources such as Harry Potter (Wicca, a pagan religion) have made their way into our schools and classrooms without parents even batting an eyelash, but the bible and prayer in school is forbidden?
Hello, anybody home?

The word 'occult' comes from a Latin word for 'hidden.' It is a collection of practices founded on the belief that humans can tap into a supernatural world. Once connected to this other realm, various rituals and special knowledge are used by those involved in the occult to allow a person to gain abilities, tapping into powers they wouldn't otherwise possess. These powers include controlling the mind, will or emotions of other people...same as divination or witchcraft.

Satan deceived Eve and told her that she and Adam would become "as gods" if they disobeyed God. Eve soon discovered she had been deceived. The serpent had lied to her. Likewise, New Age occultists are educating the masses that they, too, can become "as gods" *through meditation, divination and spiritual enlightenment.*

The underlying theme in every counterfeit religion is SELF sufficiency, becoming like God, which we know is Satan's loftiest desire. Hello? We can't even change ourselves!
I wouldn't discover till years later that because of my seemingly "innocent" curiosity with darkness, Satan would gain a legal foothold, acquiring a strategic plan for my personal life whether I consciously sought to be involved with him or not.
Ezekiel depicts Satan as created in perfection. a "covering cherub," with the intimate access to God and one who guarded His glory holiness. Ezekiel 10:1-14).

Walking "in the midst of the stones of fire" conveys a close vicinity to God just beneath the glory at the footstool of God (Ezekiel 1:27), where he would learn how to imitate God.

According to researchers with the National Study of Youth and Religion (NSYR), in a nationally representative survey of more than 3,000 U.S. teenagers' teens confess that they are open to believing in psychics, astrology, and communicating with the dead. Startling!!! More startling is that a recent Barna research finding indicates sadly that over 40% of born-again Christian's deny the existence of a literal Satan or hell and only 40% of believers acknowledge that the Holy Spirit actually" speaks' ' to them personally. I guess that might explain the absolute lack of discernment and power in the Body of Christ today!

Any attempt on our part to reach out to occult, or spiritual forces in hopes of predicting the future or supernatural advice is akin to opening up the front door and inviting Satan to move in, regardless of whether or not we believe in his existence.

Satan also leads the world astray through an educational system that teaches our children evolution, attempting to conceal the fact that God created this vast and wonderful universe.

Even in Catholic school we were taught evolution. I still recall the poster of the evolution of apes hanging up on that chalkboard! Explain that one!

Talk about an oxymoron…..

Today, Satan is working overtime in his attempt to lead humanity in rebellion against the God of the Bible. However, he knows that his time is short, and the rapture of the church is quickly approaching. If you don't believe that fact PLEASE educate yourself on bible prophecy.

We are currently in the church age of "grace," immediately before the Rapture where Jesus Christ Raptures His bride (the church) and the seven years of tribulation will follow.

The Bible tells us that no man knows the day or the hour (Matt 24:36), but we do know by current events lining up to the Bible that it is imminent. If you think this world is dark now...evil is about to intensify at warp speed.

On several websites we see that astral projection which is rooted in occultism is an essential practice of Satanists and has been around since ancient Egypt. Practicing things of the occult, sorcery or seances are not only an abomination to God, but extremely dangerous and can rapidly open you up to demons so fast that your head will literally" spin."

Ouiji Boards

It has been claimed that the 120-year-old" Ouija board", also known as a "spirit board" is used to contact the dead and communicate with departed spirits. People are so desperate to believe in a power greater than themselves seeking to gain hidden knowledge that they utilize this Hasbro tool that allows them complete access into the demonic realm.

As with astrology, it all sounds pretty harmless, but many people become intrigued, consulting the board on a regular basis, opening the door to the demonic, thus chained to its haunting long-term effects. The board is flat, marked with the letters of the alphabet, numbers 0–9, "yes", "no", "hello" and "goodbye", along with various symbols and graphics. It uses a planchette (small heart-shaped piece of wood or plastic) as a movable indicator to spell out messages during a séance. Players position their fingers on the planchette, and it moves about the board to spell out words.

The concept is to summon the departed spirits, and the demons will move the planchette around the board to spell out answers to the unknown, akin to knocking on Satan's door. The hugely popular Paranormal Activity One and Two both featured a Ouija board; while the "Exorcist" made the Ouija Board distinguishable as a "game" resulting in homicidal thoughts as it served as a mediator in allowing the devil to possess Regan, (the young girl in the movie.)

Longing to understand what happens after death is the primary reason why the Ouija board remains so popular and although mankind has made tremendous steps toward the future, we will NEVER possess the ability to see INTO the future. For this reason, we must be well acquainted with our heavenly Father; the only ONE who does.

~Reincarnation is another whacky belief that the soul, upon death of the body, comes back to earth in another body or form. ~
Ummmm. No thank you!
-And as it is appointed unto men once to die, but after this the judgment: Hebrews 9:27~

The resulting consequences of engaging in this type of activity include negative thoughts, depression, confusion, addictions and suicidal tendencies. Even Yoga has demonic roots in postures that are offered to the 330 million Hindu gods. Do a little research people. Scripture is unmistakably clear that horoscopes, psychics, tarot cards, palm readings, Ouji boards and anything else attempting to reveal the future are evil and an abomination to the Lord.

Remember that the Lord is more powerful than any satanic force and in fact created Satan, lest we forget and should we at any time encounter such evil, even through no fault of our own, summon the Lord and repeatedly declare aloud that Jesus Christ is Lord. Call upon the precious blood that has power over EVERY work of darkness and renounce the specific evil. Jesus Christ promises to forgive and deliver us of darkness and the resulting consequences of our foolish actions.

For all that do these things are an abomination to the LORD
(Deuteronomy 18:9 - 12,)

To sum it up...
NEVER open a door to the occult, or invoke dark spirits even in a playful way. Ask not, lest you be answered, Evil spirits can and do masquerade as the deceptive souls of

the departed spirits...they are called "familiar spirits."

In her book," Bringers of the Dawn "famous New Age channeler, "Barbara Marciniak actually explains away the soon Rapture by stating, "When the time comes that perhaps 20 million people leave the planet at one time there will be a tremendous shift in consciousness for those remaining." And yet in another statement, "there is a potential for many people to leave the planet in one afternoon."
You betcha...read your bible folks. It's called the Rapture of the Church, the but sadly people actually buy into this New Age stupidity at the risk of eternal damnation.
 You can't make this stuff up friends!
New agers are already preparing the masses for our lift off, "the "evolutionary purge," claiming that ALL PEOPLE WITH "BAD VIBRATIONS" will be "ejected," yep all of us Christians with bad "vibrations, "so that "Mother earth" can cleanse herself. For those of us who've been awakened

by the grace of God, it's hard to keep a straight face at this kind of foolishness, somewhat laughable but sadly the gullible steadily gravitate toward this darkness.

Seek not lest you be found, my friend. Don't joke or jest or be a pawn in the enemy's game…. your life will spiral down quickly and you'll never be the same. Satan was never intended to be our information source and if he's yours, you better bet there's a hefty payoff for him.

Bottom line: God rules!
Satan fools…
Don't let that fool be you!!!

The song remains the same:
Gen 3:1
Now the serpent… said to the woman, "Did God really say, 'You must not eat from any tree in the garden'?"
Genesis 3:13

*Then the Lord God said to the woman, "What is this you have done?" And the woman said, "The serpent deceived me and I ate." (Genesis 3:13)
Traditionally known as the blame game.
"You cannot drink the Lord's cup and the cup of demons. You cannot participate at the table of the Lord and at the table of demons."
1Conrinthians 10:21
"You were once darkness, but now you are light in the Lord. Live as children of light." (Ephesians 5:8)*

He has rescued us from the dominion of darkness and brought us into the kingdom of the Son he loves." (Colossians 1:13)

Chapter Nine: Souled out

Throughout history, many famous people have attributed their success to the simple fact that they've made a deal with the devil or "sold" their souls; including Katy Perry, Easy-E, Jay Z and Beyonce just to name a few. Do your own research. You might be surprised how many soul sellers are out there.

2 Corinthians 4:4 tells us that Satan is the god of this world, the enemy who controls the world, in part, through the influence of demon-possessed, Luciferian worshippers such as: Anton LaVey,, (author of the satanic bible,} Alice Baily, Madame Blavatsky, Albert Pike, and Aleister Crowley,(founder of the occult religion, Thelema, "do what thou wilt"), the list is endless.

Countless people of influence in pop culture in recent decades have expressed interest in

Crowley's "religion," among them Jimmy Page, Kanye West, Timothy Leary and Lady Gaga. Just as Christians look to the Holy Spirit for spiritual guidance, so do occultists look to the writings of Luciferians who are often tied to the Illuminati and actually believe that Satan is a hero or somehow good. The Bible speaks clearly about this artificial assembly. "Woe to those who call evil good and good evil; that put darkness to light, and light to darkness, that put bitter for sweet and sweet for bitter! Isaiah 5:20

Beyonce is just one of many celebrities who has freely admitted to being demon possessed and worshipping Satan. During an interview she stated, "Right before I performed for the BET awards, I raised my hands up and it was the first time I felt something else come into me. I knew that was going to be my coming out night at the award show." Her words, not mine.

"Okay people, this kind of activity has a name...demonic possession!!!
Hello, Anybody home?

Although she has never described herself as a "witch,' her former drummer accused her of practicing "extreme" witchcraft. She has even dressed up as the Yoruba deity, "Oshun" going so far as incorporating her Yoruba rituals into her visual album, "Lemonade."

Then, we have the controversial Bill Gates: On 4-10-20 Microsoft's YouTube channel debuted an advertisement video for a collaboration with Marina Abramovic, featuring her newest work, "The Life," with his mixed reality headset, "The HoloLens 2." By Sunday night there were 7,000 dislikes, and 50,000 views before the comments were deleted and disabled. On Monday, Microsoft deleted the video.

While Microsoft touts Abramovic as "the worlds most acclaimed performance artist, the 73-year-old Abramovic is best known for "spirit cooking" and is well known amongst political and Hollywood elites as the puppet mistress behind what's trending. Her performances focus on pain, blood, rituals and has included cakes that are shaped like bodies, yet Abramovic is quick to state, "I'm an artist, not a Satanist."

Wikileaks revealed in 2016 some disturbing emails between her and former Clinton campaign manager, John Podesta, (who had donated money to her institute) requesting his presence at one of the many "spirit cooking" dinners. Footage of Abramovic cutting into cakes which look astonishingly like human bodies covered in blood has gone viral. Interestingly enough, Aleister Crowley was reportedly the first to come up with spirit cooking, and "cakes of light."

There's a lot more that I won't go into great detail about, but the fact that Abramovic paints with blood, lays down in a five-pointed star (also known as Pentagram,} and has an image of herself holding a bloody ram's horn in the 2014 edition of Vogue magazine is suspect enough for me. If it walks like a duck and quacks like a duck, chances are…. You're catching on! Scooping fake blood sauce off of a woman's *naked body at the Watermill benefit auction isn't what I'd call normal, nor is the "performance artist's" recent video with the naked Lady Gaga. Do the research and decide for yourself.*

Satan certainly works overtime to deceive the masses through the entertainment industry while impressionable youngsters blindly idolize these perverted entertainers, hungering for similar experiences.

Remember the 2015 Grammys opening with AC/DC's" Highway to hell," Madonna's grand appearance wearing devil horns and Illuminati symbolism, and how about the NFL Superbowl halftime shows? This year, "Weekend" put on a grand demonic show, descending as a dark angel, with a choir of demons, for over 25,000 while others, (many children) sat glued to their TVs watching these representatives of Satan attempting to normalize demon worship.

Has it ever occurred to you that perhaps there's something or someone demonic operating this spiritually polluted puppetry leading the masses like the Pied Piper? What's alarming is that the masses who worship these diabolical performances and performers are often accompanied by impressionable teenagers who desperately long be what they see…. HELLO?

It really shouldn't be news to anyone paying even the slightest bit of attention that as time progresses, Hollywood and the music industry are obsessed with Illuminati, satanism, mysticism, occultism and now, the dreaded cannibalism.

Katy Perry's rendition of" Dark Horse" alluded to witchcraft and involved blasphemous and openly demonic dances during her 2015 Super Bowl performance and during an interview she confessed that she sold her soul to the devil. Whether she did or didn't isn't really the issue here, it's the tragic fact that she would even utter such evil, or steer her young. loyal fans down such a convoluted path. Ironically enough, a federal court ordered Katy Perry to *pay $2.78 million to Christian hip-hop artist Flame and two co-authors for allegedly stealing elements of their 2009 song "Joyful Noise" for that very song," Dark Horse,", but the judge overturned that unanimous jury decision. You be the judge. Listen and see for yourself.*

Remember, anything God does, Satan loves to imitate and pervert, for this very reason he was booted out of heaven. Satan was originally one of God's angels, created by Him to carry out His will, but became filled with jealousy and pride, and decided to lead a rebellion against God so he could take God's place as the ruler of all creation. Almost laughable, but true.

Yes, indeed the devil DOES have something of value to offer whomever he wishes. If he had the nerve to offer it to Jesus, what makes you think that you're exempt?

~Isaiah 14:13-14, "You said in your heart... 'I will make myself like the Most High'"
~Matthew 4:9

And he said to Him, "All these things I will give You if You will fall down and worship me."

A more recent display of such blasphemy is Ariana Grande's "God is a woman."
Nice try Satan!
In one image, Grande sits atop a globe, moving her fingers throughout weather charts, causing hurricanes as she dips her fingers below the surface. In another, she holds what looks like an oversized gavel. (symbol of judgement) beneath her legs, with rays of light emanating from their center. Blasphemy!
She delivers a monologue performed by Madonna, as she recites a passage of scripture from Ezekiel 25:17. "And I will strike down upon thee with great vengeance and furious anger those who attempt to poison and destroy my sisters. And you will know my name is the Lord when I lay my vengeance upon you." How are people even remotely OK with this? How do they

even sleep at night, or allow their children access to such evil?

Everyone has witnessed Tom Brady's success as a quarterback but did you know that his wife, Gisele is a self-proclaimed paganistic "good witch?"' Hello! We know that ANY witch is evil, nothing "good" about it.

Indeed, success often comes with a price. In Brady's own words, "I have these little special stones and healing stones and protection stones and she has me wear a necklace and take these little drops she makes and say all these mantras." Interesting to say the very least! She also has him go through weekly pregame rituals and according to a 2015 article in USA today, Brady keeps a four-inch bronze idol of the Hindu god "Ganesh" in his locker to reportedly, "remove all obstacles." Ganesh, the elephant headed, "god of the people" is said to bring prosperity and wealth. Again, we see how net worth is often connected to pleasing the enemy, whether it be conscious or unconscious. Giselle is Brazilian and we know that Santeria, divination and witchcraft is huge in Latin America. While you're at it, look at the last 5 or 6 Superbowl half times, demonic at it's very core.

Hollywood traditionally portrays Satan as powerful in psychological horror films such as," The Devil's Advocate`` or" extremely evil in movies like" The Exorcist" or" The Shining," focusing on mental, emotional, and psychological states to frighten, disturb, and unsettle its audience, but the Bible tells us in 1Corinthians 10:21
"You cannot drink the Lord's cup and the cup of demons. You cannot participate at the table of the Lord and at the table of demons.

Chapter Ten:

Altered States

Citizens of the US have stood by in horror as thirty-three states have decriminalized medical marijuana with some even legalizing magic mushrooms. Beyond that, unexpected drugs such as ecstasy (MDMA), psilocybin (magic mushrooms or LSD), ayahuasca, peyote (mescaline), and kratom (mitragyna speciosa) have already entered the medical research literature.

In fact one company, Minerco,Inc. (OTC:MINE) is emerging as the world's first publicly traded company focused on the research, production and distribution of psilocybin mushrooms boasting claims of its power to heal such conditions as PTSD, depression, addiction, and epilepsy. What????

Psychedelic drugs are linked to demonic influence, spiritual oppression and are a false foundation to spiritual security often propelling one into a lifetime of chaos. Many people are terrified by its damaging effects, while others embrace this new spiritual" awakening" with open arms. These seekers attempt to" escape" an unacceptable reality at any cost, opening up their souls to the demonic in exchange for the promised temporary camouflage of freedom. The drugs produce perceptions of spiritual experience, but are ultimately are tricks of the mind.

These are counterfeit spiritual experiences, offering counterfeit benefits." Spiritual warfare is very real and the enemy can strike anywhere, especially in an altered state of consciousness.

The Apostle Paul exhorts us to be sober minded and vigilant, and Peter gives us warnings about the Devil being ready to pounce at a moment's notice. Given that, it seems reasonable to say that losing your capacities (whether it be through alcohol, marijuana, or drugs) leaves you incredibly vulnerable to attack. I have personally witnessed, as a drug rehab nurse the tormenting aftereffects of LSD long after use has stopped.

Flashbacks recur without warning and may persist indefinitely, visual trails, persistent psychosis, altered sensory and perception, are just a few of the lasting effects to the seeker's high. Like dark clouds hover; another hallucinatory trip looms, without warning, lasting from a few minutes to a few hours. leaving the seeker spiritually vulnerable in a spiritual world that God absolutely forbids contact with. The devil will attempt to keep people from Christ any way he can, while he still can.

It has only been by God's amazing grace that I was personally kept from lasting consequences of my own curiosity with psychedelics in my teenage years. I have learned that there is no greater ecstasy than being safe in the heavenly Father's grace, forgiveness and perfect love.

The definition of 'pharmakeia' according to New English Translation Bible notes is: "On the term φαρμακεία (farmakeia, "magic spells") "the use of magic, often involving drugs and the casting of spells upon people – 'to practice magic, to cast spells upon, to engage in sorcery, magic, sorcery."

The Bible addresses drug use in the context of witchcraft (Gal. 5:20, Rev. 9:21 & 18:23)

Free will is God's greatest gift to mankind. If you're selling your soul for a cheap thrill or buzz, run to the MOST HIGH; where you can be assured that "ecstasy" is the real thing!

***Soul tied

I wouldn't recommend selling your soul to any person either, as far as that goes…

…Usually when people refer to a soul tie, they are referring to an emotional attachment resulting from a serious relationship with another. Close relationships can be healthy or unhealthy: In the Bible, King David and

Jonathan had a good soul tie as a result of a good friendship (1 Samuel 18:1, "And it came to pass, when he had made an end of speaking unto Saul, that the soul of Jonathan was knit with the soul of David, and Jonathan loved him as his own soul,), but tormenting soul ties can and do form from bad relationships as well.

Unhealthy soul ties are dependent, manipulative and self-destructive. When one obsesses about the individual long after the relationship ends, believing the lie that they can't be freed from the tormenting entanglement, this is an unhealthy soul tie that must be broken.

Remember, the devil will always attempt to speak lies over us, through insensitive people, teachers, authority figures and especially through our very own thoughts but those lies have absolutely no power unless we believe & and receive them as truth.

If you've been believing lies about yourself, simply allow the Holy Spirit to expose them and illuminate the Truth. Renounce the lies and move forward.

Read the Scriptures and discover your TRUE identity in Christ. Soul ties remain only when we continue to believe and feed lies. When we reject the lies and embrace the truth of God's Word, the soul ties are broken.
Acknowledging our unhealthy past sins, avoiding persons in question and asking for the perseverance to move forward is all that God requires.
~ To demonstrate the deadly sentence of one said soul tie…. ~
Steven Hoffenberg quoted that," Jeffrey Epstein sold his soul to Leslie Wexner for several billion dollars of investment in 1986." That exchange obviously didn't turn out so well.

Jeffrey Epstein, the accused sex trafficker and financier who committed suicide in a Manhattan jail in August 2019 owned a 70 acre private island, near St. Thomas, "Little St. James", where he sex trafficked and targeted *underage girls with a history of abuse and neglect, luring them to the island and authorities did NOTHING to prevent it! The unusual circumstances of his death, coupled with his wealth and friendships to essential people, have long fueled conspiracy theories surrounding his death. According to the Federal Bureau of Investigation, NCIC;In the United States, alone, an estimated 460,000 children are reported missing every year.*

Where are they? Have you ever heard about Satanic ritual abuse? It's horrific to think about, but we must.

Satan will one day be eternally assigned his place in the lake of fire, as will all of his followers (Revelation 20:15), but presently the Bible warns us to," stay alert and watch out for your great enemy, the devil prowls around like a roaring lion, seeking someone to devour." 1Peter5:8 Don't let that" someone" be you! "Our struggle is not against flesh and blood but against the powers of this dark world." (Ephesians 6:12)

Chapter Eleven:

Satan takes the stage

Without a doubt the music and film produced by Hollywood are designed to corrupt the masses, luring them away from faith in a living God, and ultimately destroying society and this planet as we know it.

Reportedly artists sign contracts in their own blood, and take oaths to serve the Satanic" brotherhood" receiving their messages via" channeling" or" alter egos" when they perform. They've clearly become victims of demonic possession. Some knowingly, some completely blindsided.

Top artists in the Satanic movement openly flaunt their allegiances, often performing blood rituals, masses and unholy ceremonies on stage *with performances consisting of literal satanic rituals conveying hidden messages to the clueless masses. Opening a door to this realm is strictly forbidden by God, yet the enemy presents the haunting song lyrics and demonic imagery as harmless and appealing to the flesh.*

Satan desperately wants to be worshipped and we know that ONLY God Almighty has that privilege! Before the fall of Satan, we know that he served as an angel before the Lord, (Ezekiel 28:14). He led worship, (HELLO) and was described as the "anointed guardian cherub." Some scholars believe he had another significantly distinguishable gift as a musical being. Only God knows the details but it's abundantly clear that there is a raging spiritual battle between the forces of God and Satan, not only in music, but in all of society.

Ezekiel 28 verse13 gives us a better look:

...the workmanship of thy tabrets and of thy pipes was prepared in thee in the day that thou wast created. Perhaps when the Archangel Lucifer spoke, it would be akin to hearing to angelic music. If he had actual pipes within him, it stands to reason that his voice sounded heavenly. His chief desire is to overthrow God and destroy mankind who is created in the image of God and be worshipped himself. John 10:10

Whether these performers admit that they're promoting and worshipping Satan or not, is totally irrelevant....

Billy Eilish-(one of the artists who performed at the 2020 democratic convention) and also recorded, "All the good girls go to hell" has currently 177 million YouTube views but she offers the twisted explanation that the videos refer to" the impact of global warming" ... really? Likely story Satan!

Sadder is the fact that people really buy that garbage...hook, line and sinker, while opening the dangerous door to the demonic, and letting their children walk in.

Eilish's frequent references to the devil are shocking and blasphemous! " She'll want the devil on her side" and "My Lucifer is lonely" are clearly Satanic. Where exactly global warming fits into her agenda is a mystery to me. Who but the devil would refer to God as a" she," mock Jesus Christ, portray hell as something to be desired, and wear a crown of spiders?
Despite her totally wicked and irreverent lyrics, she has a large, young, impressionable fanbase and whether intentional or not, she is leading millions of teenagers to the edge of a very frightening future as they innocently open that door.

With over 15 million Instagram followers, she has deemed it" entertainment" to have her controversial angel fall from heaven, land in a tar pit, and haughtily stroll away as the world burns behind her on YouTube. Where are the parents by the way? Parent is a VERB as well as a noun.

Madonna's Illuminati Facebook page has 3.4 million likes, illustrating exactly how curious people are to possess" special" enlightenment. If you explore religious content in secular music, it is shocking to find that Satan is praised and God is grossly attacked. Did you ever wonder why that is? Right! You're getting the picture. Because, just as it was in the beginning, Satan takes excessive delight in glorifying himself in his senseless attempt to dethrone the one and only TRUE God. Impossible and idiotic feat to say the least.

Another recent example is Busta Rhymes newest," The Wrath of God," released just October 30th, of this year. Hmmm...Devil's night, a coincidence! I think not! The lyrics and YouTube video to" The prophecy will be fulfilled," are so satanic and blasphemous that I refuse to make reference. Pure evidence that Satan doesn't even attempt to hide anymore.

Google will pull it up if want to take a look. Don't say I didn't warn you.
Busta Rhymes claims to be Islamic and there is much speculation that he is a "5 percenter," or member of the Nation of Gods and Earths. Busta has admitted that exposure to the Nation of Gods and Earths at a young age got him initially interested in Islam–and he seems to know a lot about the 5 percenters but one can only speculate his character by glancing at the lyrics to his songs….

"Struttin like a god"
Listen; I am the sun, I am the sea
I am the land, I am the tree
I'm everything you want to be
Cause I be struttin' like a G.O.D
Cause I be struttin' like a G.O.D
Cause I be struttin' like a G.O.D
   Wait a minute…. isn't that EXACTLY what Satan does...attempt to imitate our true God? Just saying!

Members of the group call themselves Allah's Five Percenters, which reflects the concept that ten percent of the people in the world know the truth of existence, and those elites and their agents opt to keep eighty-five percent of the world in ignorance while the remaining five percent are those who know the truth and are determined to enlighten the eighty-five percent. How pompous and prideful... Remind you of anyone?

Despite Satan's high rank in God's presence, he turned against the Lord in pride: "You said in your heart," I will ascend to heaven; above the stars of God, I will set my throne on high; I will sit on the mount of assembly in the far reaches of the north; I will ascend above the heights of the clouds; I will make myself like the Most High" (Isaiah 14:13-14)

More insulting is that" The Nation of Gods and Earths" cultivates the belief that black people are the original people of the planet enlightened by a set of principles created by

Allah. Regardless of these" prominent "secret societies, God guarantees that ALL things hidden WILL indeed be revealed. Luke 8:17

Genesis 1:27 We are EQUALLY created in the IMAGE of our gracious God and He doesn't play favorites!
Romans 2:11 For there is no respect of persons with God. No favoritism or partiality! All lives matter.... Period!

Aleister Crowley (remember the spirit cooking) is one of the famously recognized leaders of a Satanist occult group and has been labeled" the wickedest man in the world." Jimmy Page, (Led Zeppelin's guitarist) was so fascinated by Aleister Crowley and his occult teachings that he obtained his prior home in Loch Ness, Scotland. Soon rumors spread that if Jimmy Page was a Satanist, consequently the entire band of Led Zeppelin must be too.

This launched the legend that if you play "Stairway to Heaven" backwards, the demonic voices would be clearly audible. Personally, I've had no ambition to try it and wouldn't recommend it. Let's just leave it at that.

Although black magic, witches and the Devil are often viewed as symbols of Halloween, for some it's just a regular part of life. Satanic rituals, witchcraft, voodoo and occult characteristics have been embraced by these musicians as natural, and although this doesn't guarantee that they were intentionally worshipping Satan, you can bet that he was behind each lyric and tune of Black Sabbath, Ozzy Osbourne and David Bowie just to name a few.

David Bowie speculated and for good reason I'm sure, that Satan was living in his indoor swimming pool. According to his ex-wife Angie's memoir, David was fascinated with UFO's and aliens and had seen Satan rising up out of the water one night and desperately needed the pool exorcised. The exorcism left a permanent mark on the bottom of the pool resembling a beast likened to a gargoyle that reportedly, to this day still exists.

Satan leaves a mark in our lives that only the blood of Jesus Christ can permanently erase.

The god of this age has blinded the minds of unbelievers, so that they cannot see the light of the gospel of the glory of Christ, who is the image of God." (2 Corinthians 4:4)

A quick Google search will reveal the multitude of musicians and artists having been recruited to make a deal with Satan in exchange for fame and fortune. There is documented evidence and lengthy testimony how Luciferian leaders have literally reached out to the musicians through their representatives and instructed them that if they would simply sell their souls to Satan, they would become famous and quickly rise to the top of the charts and sadly, following like the Pied Piper, a multitude has taken that bait!

Ozzy Osbourne has featured the pagan god, Pan, on his album covers of Ozzfest since 2000. Pan is revered by witches, Satanists, and occultists globally and referred to as the most infamous Satanist of the 20th century.

Are you aware of the history of the artists whose music you cherish?

Do you even know the words to your favorite songs? It would certainly benefit you to invest a little time. You might be astounded to discover who inspired your "favorite" bands and exactly where those catchy lyrics originated.

Remember: the devil is always in the details!

Chapter Twelve:

Lockdown…

The Disease

I remember as a child wanting to go out and play, in search of a friend to help brighten up my day. I recall the feelings of loneliness, of wanting to fit in, so I denied what I knew to be right and entered into sin.

I began to feel really ugly and dirty from within, How I wish I'd never begun this fatal game called sin. In my ignorance I wasn't aware that my condition was from birth, a disease spreading everywhere, infecting the whole earth.

Only the blood of Jesus could stop this fatal plague.

"My friend," I ask, ``for YOUR disease, have you been washed and saved?"

The world is a prison and we are all sentenced to death
~BUT GOD!!!!

2020's new words: Pandemic, Coronavirus, COVID-19 19, lockdown, quarantine, social distancing, social conditioning, vaccinate, asymptomatic, black lives matter, sanitize, algorithms, 5-G, mask, Antifa, pansexual, gender fluid, cancel culture.
What????

Shut down, flattening the curve, PPE, Teladoc, N-95, contact tracing, Insurrection Act and the list goes on….
Stop the madness!

Nations across the world are taking drastic action in response to this created crisis: mass quarantines; school closures; sweeping travel bans restaurant, movie and let's not forget church closures. We mask up, wash hands, follow" proper" protocol, mortified that we'll be the next" victim," while vaccine makers worldwide are exempt from legal prosecution in connecting to injuries or deaths caused by the supposed "cure" to the Coronavirus.

Despite what the media portrays, many of us find that the drastic measures taken are oddly extreme. There is a hidden agenda working behind this demonic frenzy causing us to rightly," question and even rebel" against authority, because based on the most current data, the odds of actually dying from Covid-19 is .024%.

Everyone is mortified of dying of this disease, when the fact of the matter is that sin was what brought disease and death into this world and because of THAT reason, the odds of everyone dying is 100%

I wouldn't discover till many years later that Satan had a strategic plan for my personal life whether I sought to be involved with him or not. A new believer has no idea whatsoever that there's a fight ahead of him if he hasn't been versed on the devil and an uninformed Christian is a joke to the powers of darkness...ever struggling to understand, yet ignorant and vulnerable to deceit. This kind of struggle is not a precondition for growth type of struggle, this struggle is merely blindness to the enemy's plan.

Hosea 4;6 My people are destroyed for lack of knowledge.

John 1:9
"If we confess our sins, He is faithful and righteous to forgive us our sins and cleanse us from all unrighteousness."

Jesus said that in order to find one's life, we must first lose it, surrender it; give it up. While my dead doctrine and selfish ambitions were quickly destroying my soul, Jesus Christ had already victoriously triumphed over my sin and death and only He retained the power to resurrect my crooked path, dead dreams, and bitter attitudes. It wasn't until the stone of my own flesh was rolled away that I could see that the kingdom of God resided within me all along, and that I was in effect "cured" of my "disease."

First, I had to be shown that I never truly" left" salvation's road simply because I didn't put myself on it to begin with. Jesus Christ put me there the moment I believed. Next, I had to recognize my great poverty to appreciate how very prosperous I was.

Being the loving Father that He is, God permitted the loss of what I deemed valuable in this life that I might discover the immeasurable value of His love.

Isaiah 45:3 And I will give thee the treasures of darkness and hidden riches of secret places that thou mayest know that I the Lord which called you by name am the God of Israel.

Certainly, my life's "spankings" hurt Him more than they could've ever hurt me and I will praise Him throughout all of eternity for allowing me to fall.

~ If you still think that your behavior limits or defines God's love for you, child of God, you are deceived and under the bondage of performance orientation. Our works or lack of them has nothing at all to do with salvation or the Father's unconditional love for us, despite Satan's malicious doctrine to the contrary.

Satan is fully aware that he can't take our soul's eternally, so he succeeds in drawing many" church folk" away into the emotional drudgery of" performance".

Although I had abandoned the idea of "church," I found myself conveniently pushing the idea of sin further and further into my very confused soul, finding myself in the company of those who believed as I did. Amazingly, we had all come to the unspoken agreement that "sin", this absolute powerlessness and recklessness that was killing us was actually "fun", something to be "proud" of, antics worthy of public display.

Yet the very presence of sin in my daily life overwhelmed me (compliments of the Holy Spirit,) my powerlessness over it terrified me, so I kept running, looking back occasionally, always certain that it was growing larger and closer than ever, and I knew that if it ever caught up with me, I'd be permanently immobilized.

I could almost hear it mocking me, laughing at me, challenging my very being. I thought that even if perhaps there was a cure to this" disease", it was certainly beyond my grasp. Although outwardly I appeared to have it somewhat together,

I knew deep inside that sin had become bigger, stronger and faster than expected, propelling me to participate in activities I knew were destructive. My turn for death was fast approaching and I wasn't sure if I could escape its fierce grip. If only I had known back then that my feelings of failure as a human being were reinforced by the root of shame already planted in childhood, permitting the voice of" you'll never be good enough" to get louder and louder with each passing day.

Today, when I look back at it, I can plainly remember the sarcasm of the enemy. "How long are you going to run, girl, aren't you getting tired yet? You'll never stop this vicious cycle of sin. Why not give up, now?"
Reluctantly, I'd agree with the lies, allowing this invisible enemy to lead my broken soul to the outermost edges of darkness. Attributing this to gross lack of spiritual knowledge, I nearly gave up my birth rights and forfeited my identity in my Father's kingdom, but instantaneously, when I

determined in my heart that I couldn't possibly arise from these crippling conditions and that life wasn't worth the fight, the Son of God reached His hand down for me and said, "Arise, my child, your Redeemer lives."

My spirit had always known His power, but my mind, will and emotions remained imprisoned and clueless until I exhausted ALL of my own foolish human resources.

Think of addiction as a boxing ring. Once you're out of it and presumably "clean" you're finally on the outside looking in. You've been delivered from that lifestyle. You can see the blood on the faces of other boxers in that ring, but it's no longer your face that's taking the punch. By the grace of God, you're now a spectator in this brutal journey called addiction. You're making sober, healthy choices but if you willingly and foolishly step back into that boxing ring and vicious cycle of sin, the blood will be back on YOUR face, YOU will be feeling the pain and this time it just could be a TKO. Don't risk your life for something that Jesus Christ died to deliver you from completely.

Lack of knowledge, reduces us to helpless passengers in speeding vehicles that we no longer want to be riding in, placing us in frightening boxing rings that we can't find our way out of. Are you ready to jump out before it's too late? Don't let the enemy put you in a spiritual "checkmate." The game is finished, remember? The King on our board is forever immovable!

Bottom line...The ONLY vaccine to the" disease" of sin is the blood of Jesus Christ.

Chapter Thirteen:

Holiday prey

~Evil walks amongst us yet we open up our doors, to the little ghosts and goblins in groups of three and four.

 Standing with open buckets, politely chanting" trick or treat", waiting for the candy their hands are soon to meet.~

Standing right behind them are parents without a clue…. this day is not at all about candy my friend...Satan's joke is all on you! ~

    There you have it! Although most of us are guilty of "innocently" participating in cavity inducing Halloween events at one time or *another, it's definitely NOT ok to dress up as a witch or ghost and accompany our frightened, impressionable children into yards with open graves and dead bodies lying in a ditch. Wake up and smell the coffee people! Halloween is not a holiday to celebrate, it's a rush of twisted satanic indulgence that opens up more doors to "tricks" than "treats."*

The tender, pliable heart of a child is subject to what WE deny or allow into their lives and introducing Satan as a tender-hearted companion is beyond foolish.

Halloween is a night that Satanists smile at, promoting demonic fantasies, offering candied indulgence with great expectation that this forbidden taste of curiosity will later quench for that child, an insatiable appetite into darkness.

Why entertain or participate or God forbid have knowledge of allowing our children to participate in prankish nonsense such as "Devil's Night, October 30," when God has created each and every day for His own glory? Satan doesn't get any days on my calendar!

Devil's night dates from as early as the 1940s and is a night when people engage in a night of minor pranking or vandalism (such as toilet paper decorating or throwing eggs at houses and cars.) Such mischief isn't a game and escalates rapidly causing untold damages such as arson, theft murder, and untold destruction. Once again: Satan came to steal, kill, and destroy...fitting scenario. John: 10:10

Christmas and Easter...the two pivotal events in Christianity are utilized by Satan to distract the masses on the birth and resurrection of Jesus Christ with Santa Claus and Easter bunnies. Children learn more about gifts and candy than the manger and the cross, a complete mockery of our Savior's birth, death, burial and resurrection.

If you think about it, Satan & Santa share the exact same letters.
NOT just a Strange coincidence!

Santa wears red.., Jesus shed red blood.
Santa has elves...God has angels
Children Sit on Santa's lap...
Jesus said," let the little children come to me."
Santa lives in the north pole… (a fictional place,)
God lives in heaven (a very real place.)

    Most importantly Santa knows if you've been bad or good: his gifts are always conditional to a child, as depicted in the highly popular 1934 Christmas song, "Santa Claus is coming to Town"
"He knows if you've been bad or good so be good for goodness sake."
God's gift of His Son, Jesus Christ is totally unconditional because we're ALL lost in sin and none "righteous" in God's eyes without receiving His eternal gift.
 Romans 3:23 All have sinned and fallen short of the glory of God."
Romans 3:10 "As it is written, there is NONE righteous, no, not one"

HMMM. The church as well as Santa plays a huge part in the subtle indoctrination into "performance orientation", or "works." Interesting!

In God's eyes "the entire performance" was completed at the cross when Jesus Christ said, "It is finished." Can we honestly expect our children to believe in a God they can't see, when we lied about the Santa they could see? Talk about a double standard!

A sense of betrayal is inevitable when children discover they've been duped. Personally, I found out at six years of age when I spotted "Santa," aka "my stepdad" piling presents under the tree. I was so devastated that I excitedly shared it with my two-year-old brother, receiving a spanking as one of my "gifts" that year.

In the United States, Santa Claus is often depicted as a magical, famous "deliverer," flying in his magic sleigh with reindeers on Christmas Eve to deliver toys to the "good" children.

In "Santa Claus is coming to Town":
"He's making a list, "(as does God, more commonly known as "The Lamb's Book of Life)
And checking it twice;
Gonna find out Who's naughty and nice (conditional love)
He knows if you've been bad or good
So be good for goodness sake!"

Come on now...being "good," for presents, with a primary motivation of fear isn't really a virtue to instill in our children.

By all accounts, Santa's story begins in the fourth century AD in what is now modern-day Turkey. A man named Nicholas became the bishop of a village called Myra. He was later canonized, and soon became one of the most popular saints in Christianity. The name Santa Claus is derived from Sinterklaas which is derived from Saint Nicolaas.

This pagan tradition has come to signify indulgence, dishonoring the meaning of Christmas altogether. A visit from St. Nicholas", more commonly known as "The Night Before Christmas" was published anonymously in 1823, later attributed to Clement Clarke Moore, who claimed authorship in 1837.

"But an unknown source penned this heartfelt version. Although Jesus Christ did indeed come as a baby, He will soon return to rapture the church, His glorious bride.

~'Twas the night before Jesus came~

'Twas the night before Jesus came and all through the house
Not a creature was praying, not one in the house.
Their bibles were lain on the shelf without care
In hopes that Jesus would not come there.

The children were dressing to crawl into bed.
Not once ever kneeling or bowing a head.
And Mom in her rocker with baby on her lap

Was watching the Late Show while I took a nap.

When out of the East there arose such a clatter,
I sprang to my feet to see what was the matter.
Away to the window I flew like a flash
Tore open the shutters and threw up the sash!

When what to my wondering eyes should appear
But angels proclaiming that Jesus was here
With a light like the sun sending forth a bright ray
I knew in a moment this must be THE DAY!

The light of His face made me cover my head
It was Jesus! returning just like he had said.
And though I possessed worldly wisdom and wealth,
I cried when I saw Him in spite of myself.

In the Book of Life which He held in His hand.
Was written the name of every saved man.

He spoke not a word as He searched for my name;
When He said "It's not here" my head hung in shame.

The people whose names had been written with love
He gathered to take to His Father above.
With those who were ready He rose without a sound.
While all the rest were left standing around.

I fell to my knees, but it was too late;
I had waited too long and thus sealed my fate.
I stood and I cried as they rose out of sight;
Oh, if only I had been ready tonight.

In the words of this poem the meaning is clear;
The coming of Jesus is drawing near.
There's only one life and when comes the last call
We'll find that the Bible was true after all!

- *Imagine how you would feel if people all over the world celebrated your birthday and neglected to invite you.*

Bottom line...
Satan is a liar and if you're living a lie, you're usually the last one to know.

Part three:

Full circle

Chapter Fourteen:

There's no place like home

The road leading back home to our heavenly Father's embrace will invariably differ for each prodigal. Often a prodigal has no feelings or recollections associated with the implantation of the eternal Seed into their spirits, thinking that salvation "didn't take" suffering, phenomena likened to that of spiritual amnesia. Just as a woman receives the implantation leading to conception without feeling; likewise, the mystery of being born again of the spirit by receiving the Holy Spirit.

John 3:8, Jesus says, "The wind blows where it wishes [that is the free will of the wind], and you hear its sound, but you do not know where it *comes from or where it goes. So, it is with everyone who is born of the Spirit."*

The work of the Holy Spirit in the life of a believer may or may not be seen. His work is sovereign and just as the wind blows where it wishes and we sometimes hear its sound or perceive its movement in the swaying of trees or waves in the sea we do not know where it comes from. nor do we know where it is going.

Being born of God's Spirit isn't a mystical experience reinforced by fleshly sensationalism; on the contrary, it's a fact, totally independent of human emotion. Nicodemus was a RELIGIOUS rabbi in the Bible but he wasn't born again. So that tells us one can be religious and not born again.
Let me hold my tongue...

*I could write a whole book on that topic simply from what I've personally experienced by "religious folk" in "churches," but I'll restrain myself and save it for another time! *

When Jesus says, "That which is born of the flesh is flesh, and that which is born of the Spirit is spirit," he means that we are merely human flesh and spiritually dead at our first birth because we're born into the "condition" of sin but are made spiritually alive by our second birth:(born-again into the "condition" of righteousness…His righteousness.)
John 3:6, KJV: "That which is born of the flesh is flesh; and that which is born of the Spirit is spirit.".

In the story of the prodigal son, long before the son's full admission of repentance the Father saw him in the distance and came running to meet him. The very nanosecond the son decided to forsake his prodigal lifestyle, the Father's heart was moved because he knew that the son could now appreciate the inheritance, he longed to bestow upon him. Little did that son know that the true inheritance was so much more valuable than the monetary "inheritance" he had already squandered away.

With a smile upon His face and His arms stretched open wide, the father rejoiced that his son had finally abandoned his selfish ways and "came to himself."

Unfortunately, some of us require rougher, longer journeys to lose ourselves than others and for the exact amount of time we choose to remain in captivity, the true inheritance will remain locked. Stubbornly we cling to what we believe our hearts cherish most, blindsided that the addiction or habit we cleave to is but a well-crafted tool, fashioned by the enemy for our destruction.

Being sovereign ruler of all, God fully allows the enemy, (who we know is a created being), to drive the prodigal to that very place of despair and hopelessness, where he finally admits a need for the one to whom his spirit is eternally engaged) thus arriving full circle.

With a newfound awareness of this enemy, he can now deliberately avoid the same route that brought about his destruction, seeking to warn others of the fatal grip associated with sin.

Although Satan remains successful in drawing many of us out of the Spirit to walk in the flesh, he's incapable of drawing us out of the Spirit and into eternal damnation.

Because the prodigal believes the lie that the door to eternal life has been permanently closed due to his behavior and obvious rebellion, he has become the enemy's most susceptible prey...a walking target.

Not understanding and appropriating the fact that Jesus Christ IS the DOOR, never again to be closed, they've erected a blockade that unless forcefully recognized and demolished, will obscure the truth for a lifetime.

Believing the lie that they've forfeited God's favor, and carrying the weight of false pride the prodigal sees only the impenetrable door they've erected, never the grace of God. Spiritually speaking, the door they see doesn't exist because Jesus Christ IS the door they've previously walked through at the moment of salvation. Their faulty perception of that door being closed was just that...faulty.

Revelation 3:8

"I know thy works, behold I have set before thee an open door and no man can shut it."

Breaking down the door....

Having stared at that imaginary door for ten long years, I haven't forgotten what it looked like. I am most familiar with the faulty perceptions and vicious lie that life is hopeless. I haven't forgotten the cloak of despair I donned daily...But because I was ALREADY God's own, He made a way of escape, heroically carrying me back through the same door I'd already eternally entered.

Although my wounds have been wondrously healed, and my scars nearly invisible, I retain within my hands the same oil the Master utilized to heal my broken body and soul. These are the works of my hands, and you beloved prodigal, are the treasured reward.

Grace Alone

We must run from false teachers and religions teaching that we need to add to the crucifixion and resurrection of Jesus Christ. We were birthed into the Kingdom of God the moment we said, "I do." Therefore, hold fast to that truth regardless of the depths to which you've fallen because the completed work at Calvary my friend can never be lost or retracted for any reason whatsoever. It is finished!

For by grace, you have been saved through faith, and that not of yourselves; it is the gift of God, not of works, lest anyone should boast. Ephesians 2:8-9

It comforts me to know that the I ten years I spent as a prisoner of war, suffering from near spiritual starvation, was simply preparing me for a later chapter in my life. This one!

Chapter Fifteen:
Losing my religion

Religion is but a deceptive smokescreen of safety and security wherein I never felt safe, so I've elected to lose my religion altogether. Growing up Catholic, the practice of confessing my sins to a priest made me feel naked and vulnerable and as I walked away feeling no less filthy, I truly wondered who in the world bestowed upon that "priest" the power to forgive my sins in the first place,

The Roman Catholic Church teaches that the bread and wine of the Holy Eucharist become the actual body and blood of Jesus. In A.D. 1551, the Counsel of Trent officially stated, "By the consecration of the bread and wine there takes place a change of the whole substance e of the bread into the substance of the body of Christ our Lord and of the whole substance of wine into the substance of his blood. This change the holy Catholic Church has fittingly called transubstantiation, believing that they are fulfilling John 6:53, where Jesus said, "Truly, truly I say to you, unless you eat the flesh of the Son of Man and drink his blood, you have no life in you."

I have since learned that this doctrine is totally and absolutely in error. The eucharist has nothing to do with salvation my friend, the state of grace occurred once and for all at the moment of salvation. Jesus said, "in John 6:63-64 that it is the Spirit who gives life; the flesh is of no avail, so why in the world would we have need to eat Jesus" flesh" to have eternal life? The Catholic definition of Holy Eucharist never made any sense because it's unbiblical, a re-sacrifice of Christ's sacrifice. Christ does not need to ever again be re-sacrificed. Reference Hebrews 7:7 or 1 Peter 3:18. Christ died for sins ONCE and for all, never again needing to be reoffered for sins, in direct opposite of transubstantiation, demonstrating that we receive Christ's sacrifice through faith alone! John 1:12, 3:16

As mentioned, I perceived Satan to be the harmless, silly character with horns and red suit much like the character demonstrated in the new Match.com video.

It strikes me as odd, now that I'm personally acquainted with the enemy's schemes, that his agenda remains so hidden and insignificant in "church" of all places. They don't talk too much about the rapture either, but that's a different chapter.

The Word of God tells us in 1Peter 5:8 that Satan is not only our enemy, but also our "accuser". According to the dictionary, the word accuser is defined as follows: to charge with a fault or offense....to blame. Revelation 12:10 tells us that the enemy accuses the saint's day and night before God.

When I finally became familiar with the voice of the Holy Spirit, it wasn't long before I realized that the other voice in this war was indeed that of the adversary who sought the destruction of my soul. Unwittingly, I had incorporated his subtle, hateful gestures into my everyday thinking, behavior patterns, and goals, claiming his lies as my own, fully embracing the painful arrows he'd intended for my destruction.

As long as the enemy succeeds in remaining hidden, he'll continue to entrap our wills, leading us into the seductive web of self-hatred, despair, and hopelessness, promoting nothing but self, and because he's been around a lot longer than any of us have, he's keenly aware of what appeals to the flesh.

Isn't it only natural that he'd offer a replacement, a counterfeit exchange for a living relationship with Christ in the name of" religion," assuring the saints that God is actually pleased with "works", rendering us totally useless for service because we're too busy" working?" Interesting concept...you gotta admit, to make one feel good about their" accomplishments," yet totally blindsiding them to the true work of the gospel is rather ingenious.

Another oddity I've discovered in my journey is that I never heard even one testimony as a child. Now granted, I didn't pay much attention in church back then, but I would certainly remember hearing about a life radically transformed by a miracle, simply because I was in such desperate need of one myself.

Communication of our testimony is of vital importance to the furthering of the gospel, but sadly fear prevents many Christians from testifying to Christ's wonder-working power so relevant to the gospel.

Since I've been back in the church, I often hear people say, "Oh, you don't want to give Satan any glory by going into details about your life."

What!

I can almost see the enemy sitting in the front pew laughing.

The word of our testimony is one of our most powerful weapons available for victory in Christ; as well as a tool utilized by God to feed His missing sheep and draw them back into the fold. Although I'm certainly not proud of the heights from which I've fallen, I can assure you that my opportunities for "true ministry" have been multiplied by my transparency and willingness to expose "the enemy's hidden agenda." I don't call that "glorifying" Satan, I call it exposing the deceptive mind behind the wicked schemes of my Fathers defeated foe.

Revelation 12:11 And they overcame him by the blood of the Lamb, and by the word of their testimony; and they loved not their lives unto the death.

People struggling with sin don't want to hear how "holy" or "anointed" Christians are because it makes them feel even more inferior, more intimidated than they already feel.

A sinner already condemned by the weight of their sin doesn't need to be reminded of what they already so desperately know.

We need to communicate that we as Christians are absolutely approachable, made holy by the blood of Jesus ALONE.

Hosea 4:6 my people are destroyed for lack of knowledge...

My heart also breaks to witness certain groups of people choosing to define God as" they understand him," reducing our Creator to a level where they determine what's acceptable to Him based upon their own doctrine.

Worshiping a God of our own convenient understanding is absolutely meaningless when it's not defined by truth, denoting that we actually place our faith in our own understanding; a dangerous practice, indeed. God is honored by obedience and reverence to His immutable Word and because He is God, we must accept that it's HIS autonomous right to create His own standard.

All of humanity, because of sin, is excluded from living in the presence of a holy God; regardless of our works or deeds, and only those of us having entered the door of life through Jesus Christ's death on the cross have met the Father's requirements. Period!

The bible clearly states that all have sinned and fallen short of the glory of God. God's own declaration was that the wages for man's sin was death. Jesus said, "I am the resurrection and the life He who believes in me, though he dies, yet shall he live." God will not and cannot violate His own nature or Word!

Jesus Christ suffered and died on the cross to satisfy the penalty demanded by our sin, exchanging for it His own righteousness. What a deal! God never required that we change our nature to please Him. Knowing that it was impossible, He provided the only alternative…His Son.

When we agree with God and yield to His sovereign plan, His voice becomes unmistakably audible to the human spirit. When we disagree, the results can be unmistakably deadly to the wayward soul.

God is not a God of confusion!
(1Cor 14:33) For God is not the author of confusion, but of peace, as in all churches of the saints. People who play "make-believe" or take pride in living "morally correct" lives will be sadly mistaken when they stand before the Lord.

Unfortunately, even as Christians, we judge and navigate our relationship with God according to how well our flesh does or doesn't perform when it has nothing to do with the "performance" of our flesh... A welcome relief to those of us who weren't the goody two shoes of the crowd. Of course, there's the other extreme in the crowd. "I've blown it. The sins I've committed in my life are just too much for God to forgive."

Both extremes are rooted in pride. Again; the flesh. Dare we say that Christ died in vain by implying that our sin was too great for Him to forgive or dare we utter how morally correct we lived our lives, relinquishing the need for a Savior altogether, as demonstrated by Missouri Democrat. Emanuel Cleaver, while leading the House in a prayer during the swearing-in of the 117th Congress on Sunday, January 3, 2020."We ask it in the name of the monotheistic God, Brahma, and (the) God known by many names, many different faiths," he said. "Amen, and Awomen."
Say what? This my friend, is Irreverence at its worst! Someone needs to educate this "ordained Methodist minister that, "The Amen" is actually one of Jesus Christ's countless holy names.

Revelation 3:14 "To the angel of the church in Laodicea write: These are the words of THE AMEN, the faithful and true witness, the ruler of God's creation.

Steve Harvey…another celebrity sell out previously claimed to be a Christian, even toured with the now controversial Kirk Franklin, yet his constant sexual innuendos on Family Feud have always been a dead giveaway, because "out of the abundance of the heart the mouth speaks." Luke 6:45

Dressed as a Muslim along with his wife, in front of Sheikh Zayed Grand Mosque in The United Arab Emirates this year, Harvey made the statement that, "There's no one way to Heaven, no one way to Paradise. It's like television, now there are over 800 channels on cable, and they're all pretty entertaining. So, I'm pretty sure that to get to Heaven, there's got to be more than one route. Because somebody watching another channel or taking another channel than you, they're probably still getting entertained." His words, not mine!
Say what?

If all religions are correct, as long as one believes in them, as he states, then Santa and the Easter Bunny have quite the following!
Nice try Satan.

Oh, what a tangled web we weave, when we first we practice to deceive! God hasn't labelled the world as sinners because we've sinned. The fact of the matter is that we've sinned simply because we're sinners…. whether we believe that or not

For all have sinned, and come short of the glory of God; Romans 3:23

Chapter Sixteen:

The Great Deception

*In my lifetime, there has been a dramatic increase in UFO awareness, global elites, and talk of the soon coming New World Order. •

My great-grandmother spoke frequently about these things when I was growing up. She warned of the mark of the beast system, New world order, a cashless society, one world religion, increase in lawlessness, pandemics and the increasing frequency of earthquakes and climate change.

She also spoke of the fulfilled prophecy of Israel becoming a nation in 1948, the fig tree generation, and the grand delusion that the rapture would be blamed on alien abduction.

Everything I once rolled my eyes and giggled at; I am now watching unfold at warp speed progression. Satan isn't even hiding anymore in these last days. He's blending in exceedingly well in this world's toxic environment. Those of us who've been awakened by God's gracious Spirit are fully aware that he's hiding in plain sight!

One world religion:

An emerging common belief that once all the world's religions come together, a miraculous spokesman will arise….uhhhh, yeah…the Antichrist hello???.

An article published on April 3, 2019 by "Rome Reports," reveals Pope Francis speaking with an audience of Muslims, telling them that God wants a fraternity among Muslims and Catholics. Ummmm I think not!!!!How can all religions worship the same God when there's only ONE way to the Father, and that is through His Son, Jesus Christ! Dumb devil! What Bible does that Pope even read?

For there is one God and one Mediator between God and men, the Man Christ Jesus, 1 Timothy 2:5

John 14:6 Jesus said to him, "I am the way, the truth, and the life. No one comes to the Father except through Me.
"Chrislam" is a cult attempting to synchronize Christianity with Islam, hence the name "Chris" for Christ and "lam" for Islam. Its central belief is that Christianity and Islam are compatible, worship the same God, and that a person can be Christian and a Muslim at the same time. Talk about confusion. What happened to brains? If Muslims deny the resurrection of Christ on the cross, where is a Savior in all of this false teaching? Christianity teaches grace alone, by faith alone, through Christ alone. Stick with the winner...if God Himself said there's only one way…. why believe the LIAR???

One World Currency:

A cashless society describes an economic state whereby financial transactions are not conducted with money in the form of physical banknotes or coins, but rather through the transfer of digital information between the transacting. The Wall Street Journal even mentions how central banks are getting closer to issuing their own digital currency. Post-pandemic certainly looks like we're heading straight in that direction…. on the cusp of a cashless society as predicted in the Bible.

One World Government:

Globalists believe there needs to be one political authority for all of humanity, Christians already know from the Bible that this is the Anti-Christ, the one who will implement the rule that you can't buy or sell without his "mark." Currently it's, "no mask, no service, "soon to be replaced in the Tribulation with, "no mark, no service."

Collapsing the economy on purpose has certainly been part of the enemy's agenda.
New World Order
The Great Reset; catchy name for NWO, wouldn't you agree? It's a proposal by the World Economic Forum (WEF) to rebuild the economy sustainably following the COVID-19 pandemic (plan-demic) unveiled in May 2020 by the United Kingdom's Prince Charles and WEF director Klaus Schwab. Stay tuned!

The COVID-19 vaccine
Bill Gates's name is constantly being mentioned these days in connection with his interests in pharmaceutical companies, vaccines, and WHO funding. Luciferase Patent WO/2020/060606 was registered on 26 March 2020. The patent application was filed by Microsoft Technology Licensing, LLC, headed by Bill Gates, back on 20 June 2019, (before the pandemic) and, on 22 April 2020, the patent was granted international

status. The title of the patent is "Cryptocurrency system using body activity data,"

Gate's company is also involved in the digital ID project ID2020 Alliance. On the website's homepage, it says that the project has been addressing the issue of digital rights since 2016. His TED Talk from 2015 titled "The next outbreak? We're not ready" is being shared widely online since the impact of COVID-19 around the world.

Talk about foreknowledge!

Even China's role in this "pandemic" is now questionable. None of this sits right in my spirit and that's EXACTLY why God has given us the Holy Spirit. To bear witness to the truth and make us feel uncomfortable with a lie.

Let's just say that this nurse won't be taking a vaccine anytime soon, I'll stay amongst the outcasts who refuse it even if we're sure to be labeled the new lepers of society.

Aliens:

A 180-day countdown is currently underway for the Pentagon and spy agencies to reveal what they all know about UFOs. Attached to the 5,593-page coronavirus relief bill the President Trump signed in January 2021 is a startling proposition: a request for the Pentagon to brief Congress on all it knows about unidentified flying objects within the new 180-day time limit. The Plot thickens, wouldn't you say?

As far back as the 1950s, people have reported seeing Unidentified Flying Objects (U.F.O.'s) at a military base in Southern Nevada. Area 51 is a high-security, very secretive open training range for the U.S. Air Force that has become the subject of many conspiracy theories. The belief that Area 51's "military base" is a cover for alien research is reinforced by the fact, not only is it off limits to civilians but believed by paranormal enthusiasts and conspiracy theorists be a heavily guarded underground lab where the government possibly retains aliens, UFO's, and God only knows what else. This dramatic increase of UFO awareness amongst the population is a simple; satanic preparation for the rapture of the church, which he knows is imminent.

The public knows something deceptive is going on, even those who are inclined to dismiss such evidence. Those of us who have been awakened by the grace of God know without a doubt that Aliens are actually fallen angels and demons active since Biblical days. Demons are pure spirit and can appear as attractive, dreadful or assume whatever form Satan commands.

In the book of Ezekiel, Alien spacecraft have been described as discs of fire but we refer to them today as unidentified flying objects UFOs) but those who haven't read a Bible wouldn't know that this very phenomenon was long ago prophesied.

Hollywood's growing fascination with aliens, and UFO's has only intensified since the likes of Star Trek, Star Wars, Lost in space and ET: depicting aliens as friendly and for good reason. The fake media will televise the rapture as worldwide UFO abduction.

If you're still here, don't believe it!!!

The event we call "the rapture" is when God will remove his people (born-again followers of Jesus Christ) from the earth in preparation for a terrible time of judgment prepared for those who have rejected His Gift of Salvation through Jesus Christ in the coming seven-year tribulation.

Recently Haim Eshed, (former Israeli space chief and highest-ranking official in the military) notified Yediot Aharonot, an Israeli newspaper, that humans have made contact with aliens, and even formed a "Galactic Federation."

President Donald Trump was, according to the Israeli, "on the verge" of revealing the existence of aliens to the general public, but to prevent alarm, couldn't yet disclose the matter. In the very near future when the church of Jesus Christ is raptured, a reenactment might play out like that of the 1938 War of the World's hoax by Orson Welles. Only this time it won't be a hoax. We truly will have vanished, and of course the explanation will be that it was alien abduction. It's safe to say that when 200 million people vanish off of the planet, the world will take notice. I pray for your sake, that you're not left behind wondering what just transpired.

Like 15:3-7 Then Jesus told them this parable: 4 "Suppose one of you has a hundred sheep and loses one of them. Doesn't he leave the ninety-nine in the open country and go after the lost sheep until he finds it? 5 And when he finds it, he joyfully

puts it on his shoulders 6 and goes home. Then he calls his friends and neighbors together and says, 'Rejoice with me; I have found my lost sheep.' 7 I tell you that in the same way there will be more rejoicing in heaven over one sinner who repents than over ninety-nine righteous persons who do not need to repent.

Chapter Seventeen:

Dead man walking

This chapter isn't as much about "The Walking Dead" and zombies as it is about literal "Dead men walking. "For the record: The Bible states that a person's spirit is actually DEAD until it is made alive through Christ, making him literally, a dead man walking.

In Ephesians 2:1 Paul the Apostle says, "We were once DEAD in our trespasses and sins."

It wasn't until God awakened me from my spiritual amnesia and the stone of my filthy flesh was rolled away that I could see that the kingdom of God resided within me all along.

I had to first recognize my great poverty to see how rich I truly was. permitting the loss of what I deemed valuable in this life to find the immeasurable treasure of His love. I guess the *reason I feel so compelled to reach you with the details of my story is because untold millions of God's children remain deceived, buried alive in the same dead doctrines, selfish ambitions and deceptive grave clothes that I so desperately clung to. Reaching them has become the pivotal force behind my life's call.*

Everyone's story is different; some, I'm sure some more complex than others. I can only hope that you'll see beyond my personal grave and into your own.

Once again, I need to clarify that Jesus Christ is not a religion or an endless set of rules and regulations, neither is He the law, slapping us in the face with a ticket of shame each time we sinfully speed by. That's precisely the doctrine I believed and the lie responsible for my soul remaining in a self-imposed grave.

If my testimony helps even one of you to reevaluate your concept of God, or convince you that Jesus Christ came to set you free from the tyranny of manmade doctrine, perhaps I will have accomplished what He's asked of me.

If you believe that God is unreachable, you won't reach Him because you've bought the lie that He's unreachable., He's already reached us by providing Christ's perfect sacrifice for our sins. If you believe that you're unworthy; well join the club...you're finally on the right track because according to God all of us are, thus His perfect motive for the redemptive work of the cross.

If you ARE already born again, the Holy Spirit currently resides in your spirit and longs to restore fellowship to your broken soul.
If Satan can offer us his lame definition of a God who wants nothing to do with us until we die, wouldn't that immediately eradicate our kingdom positions here on earth, rendering us incapable of fulfilling God's will here and now? Think about it.

Somehow, I bought the lie that the kingdom of God was IN Heaven. Stay with me now and learn what it took me many years to understand. When Jesus said in John 3:3-5 that unless a man be born again, he cannot SEE the kingdom of God, I assumed that would only happen when I died (see the kingdom), but it literally means that "spiritually" you can't see the kingdom at all, whether you're alive or when your physical body dies simply because you haven't been spiritually born. What I neglected to see is that the kingdom of God is immediately accessible to the believer. When we are born again, we are transferred immediately from one kingdom to another. Notice how the Apostle Paul puts it in Colossians 1:13.

"He has delivered us from the domain of darkness and transferred us to the kingdom of his beloved Son," (Colossians 1:13)

In John 18:36, when Jesus said: "My kingdom is not of this world", how easy it must've been for my eleven-year-old mind to mix that up with "My kingdom is not IN this world." I thought that if His kingdom wasn't OF this world, most assuredly I had to die to see His kingdom. It made sense at the time. Such a costly error received by a child whose intention was simply to "please" God.

I did have to die alright, but only to the stubborn, rebellious self that refused to surrender my grave clothes and that transformation wouldn't occur until I became terrified of the darkness that sought to bury me alive.

If you still think that your behavior limits or defines God's love for you, child of God, you are deceived and under the bondage of performance orientation. Our works or lack of them have nothing at all to do with the Father's unchanging love for us, despite Satan's lies to the contrary.

He knows fully that he can't take our soul's eternally, but he succeeds in drawing souls away into the emotional darkness of the *performance, while their true destiny stands knocking.*

Beloved, for your sake, I pray that your tongue on earth has already confessed Him and that your heart has already believed in His saving grace when the rapture occurs.
If you think that the enemy doesn't have a voice in your soul, you had better think again.

The fact that you deny his existence doesn't make you exempt from his seductive deception, but totally qualifies you as a dead man walking, and the only remedy is the blood of his victor, Jesus Christ. People who live "morally" correct lives will be sadly mistaken when they stand before the Lord because being "good," will never be good enough. The flesh loves to take credit for any works of righteousness, but again, God said" let no flesh glory in my presence."

I don't know about you, but I'd rather hear that now, than on the day I'm standing in front of Him. Jesus said, "Unless a man be born again, he cannot enter the kingdom of heaven."

John 3:3 Jesus answered and said unto him, "Verily, verily, I say unto thee, except a man be born again, he cannot see the kingdom of God." Foolishly we navigate our relationship with God according to how well our flesh does or doesn't perform judging others by the severity of their sin when the gospel is all about grace not "performance.".

Of course, there's the other extremist. "I've blown it. The sins I've committed in my life are just too much for God to forgive." Both extremes are rooted in pride. Again; the flesh. How dare we say that Christ died in vain by saying that our sin was too great for Him to forgive or dare we think ourselves so morally correct that we didn't need a Savior in the first place.

The flesh can be so very cunning and powerful at times….so cunning it has to die….and did. God didn't label us sinners because we've all sinned...We've sinned simply because we're all sinners.

Chapter Eighteen:

Who's afraid of the big bad wolf?

    Remember the story of the three little pigs? The only house that stood firm against the fierce wind of the wolf's breath was the one made of brick.

The other two brothers had built their houses of straw and sticks only to discover their homes would soon be destroyed by the big, bad wolf. Their only refuge was to flee to the brother's house they had previously accused of wasting time as he labored intensely to secure and build his house properly.

    That wiser brother didn't condemn his brothers when he saw them running towards home, the wolf hot on their heels. No, he opened the door and sheltered them from their relentless *predator, assisting in their escape from destruction.*

If I remember correctly, it seems that together they celebrated with a song of victory proclaiming their faith to the world, singing, "Who's afraid of the big, bad wolf", remember?

That didn't stop the big bad wolf, though, did it? He was looking for a way in the house, any way at all, so he tried to force himself down the chimney, but to his dismay the brothers were inside of the house placing logs on the fire to keep it strong and mighty. It was the fiery heat of those flames that sent their enemy running, never to return again.

Isn't that how it should be in the household of faith? Shouldn't we open our hearts and doors to our prodigal brothers and sisters when we see them running towards us? If we don't extend the unconditional love of our Savior, who will?

The house that the wiser brother built, I liken to the soul of a man. The wiser brother made prudent choices throughout his life and thus secured for himself a shelter, while his siblings chose to assemble their homes out of whatever was accessible at the moment. They were too busy thinking about having fun and fulfilling the immediate lusts of their flesh with no consideration to possible long-term consequences.

Although he had never seen the wolf himself, the wiser brother trusted Father's Word with childlike faith, believing that indeed a wolf existed and undoubtedly this enemy was his greatest threat.
The fact that they are brothers undeniably makes them from the same household, having been taught the same instructions or doctrine but choosing to walk completely different paths.
So, it is for the prodigal who, as a direct result of his own poor choices, one day finds himself in the pig pen of life, despite his upbringing and training in righteousness, despite watching his brother's house so meticulously

built, brick by brick, no apparent winds of destruction or storms on the horizon.

It almost seems unfair that some of us appear to have more "hell" prevailing against us than others, doesn't it?

God alone knows the reason why a child of His, whose foundation has already been built upon the Rock, has chosen to employ the cheapest materials available to build his house, materials that he knows in his heart won't keep the wolf out.

Perhaps he feels for whatever reason that he deserves to be destroyed or worse yet walks around day after day, totally unaware that a wolf even exists. Why would he take authority over something he has no conscious awareness of?

Therefore, he builds to the best of his ability knowing full well how faulty the construction of his home is, yet remains powerless to change it. Convinced that God is mad at him (compliments of the wolf), he walks around in his familiar place of despair and torment, silently wishing things were different, yet convinces himself that life will forever be hopeless.

Memories of his "perfect" brothers occasionally cross his mind, but he quickly dismisses the thoughts.

"If only I could've been like him."

"If only I could've listened to the rules and used the materials offered me, perhaps my home wouldn't be such a mess, " he thinks as he reaches for a strong enough substance to temporarily kill the pain

The memories of his "perfect" brother will either lead him back home or be the very obstacle keeping him away, so Body of Christ, we need to be actively producing substantial memories for our brothers and sisters,

that their memories of home be good ones, should they ever find themselves in the wolf's domain,

Although I was indeed a sheep, my perception of who God was and who I was, was distorted due to lack of knowledge. Believing I had "left" the flock, I built my house with the only materials at my disposal passed down to me from family and friends and of course the "wolf" whom I was oblivious even existed, until he started huffing and puffing.

I'm sure there were times that memories of "church" crossed my mind from time to time, but I quickly dismissed them because my heart didn't envision an open door with loving arms to greet me; or a warm fireplace burning, the embrace and prayers of brothers and sisters awaiting.

Unfortunately, I saw and heard the absolute opposite and it was those very real "church" experiences that prevented my heart from traveling in that direction.

The only pigs I saw waiting at the door were the pigs of judgment and condemnation.

When God intervened on my behalf, it wasn't in a church but in my very own living room, the wolf hot on my trail, huffing and puffing and *blowing but forbidden to blow my house down because it wasn't his house.*

True, I had assembled my house with unworthy materials but God Himself was the Builder and wasn't about to let the gates of hell trespass upon His property. He alone held the title deed and legal rights to the foundation.

A bloodline was drawn around that foundation and despite the condition or contents, despite the depravity of its appearance to the outside world, my home was paid in full by the Master Architect.

Despite the fact that those passing by could see no real value in the home and some even secretly sought its demolition to make their own street look better, the BUILDER saw its value.

He knew that it would take effort to tear down the ugly walls and pull up the hideous carpeting.

He knew it would literally take years to clear out the wreckage on that property, but He also held within His hand the final blueprint and treasured it with a passion beyond measure.

He had already taken into account the costly resurrection and restoration, but paid it all on Calvary without objection.

Unfortunately for some of us that restoration won't happen until the enemy huffs and puffs hard enough that we lose what we believe to be our true value.

For some, it won't be until we find ourselves in a position where nothing BUT divine intervention will save us. ONLY then will we discover that, in losing ourselves, we finally found ourselves.

Only then do we die to a self that was created in the mind of the enemy, finally free to live the abundant life that Jesus Christ promised.

~Is YOUR house adequate to withstand the terrifying power of the wolf?

Chapter Nineteen:

Doubting Thomas

Thomas was the disciple who refused to believe that the other disciples had seen the Lord unless he himself saw the Lord's hands and the print of the nails. He said that he simply wouldn't believe unless he personally put his own hand into the Savior's side.

Jesus took Thomas' hand and gently guided his fingers into the nail print and said, "Thomas, because you have seen me, you have believed. Blessed are those who have not seen me and yet have believed." John 20:27. At that point, I'm sure Thomas was quite humbled, gladly forfeiting his fleshly doubt, in exchange for the Savior's provision.

Although you don't know me personally and may never meet me, you have my word that Jesus Christ is who He claims to be. I have purposely allowed you to touch the place of my heart's greatest sorrow and pain that you might see that Jesus Christ is still very much alive.

The opportunity for you to now believe and receive is being extended to you throughout the pages of this book. Personally, I will always be His friend and disciple, not because I need a religion or philosophy in life, but because I have always been His.

I have personally witnessed the resurrection within my own soul and am fully prepared to testify beyond any shadow of a doubt that Jesus Christ is still alive and well and able to deliver.

Our enemy, I'm certain, has gone to considerable lengths to keep this information from you and although it seems impossible to loosen his grip right now, although the pain seems all-consuming, I assure you, that if you are truly born again of God's precious Holy

Spirit, the same resurrection power that raised Jesus Christ from the grave will get you where you need to go, if you simply yield to the Truth.

That choice is now in your hands. You have everything you need for the journey back home and nothing shall be impossible to those of us who believe, for that eternal spark of wisdom abides within our spirits.

Only His truth has the power to set us free, and only our willingness to yield to that truth will cause the enemy to finally flee. The Truth, once you know it, will change everything!

Have you wandered so far that you can't return? Only if you have chosen to believe that beloved for there is no height to which any of us have fallen that the Son of God hasn't already been. 1Are you "in" Christ Jesus? I didn't say a church building, I said, IN Christ Jesus. I was "in" Christ Jesus for ten years but nowhere near a church because I "felt" condemned by God. Do you know what? God doesn't condemn those that are IN Christ Jesus.

The Holy Spirit brings conviction but God will never condemn those who already belong to Him because He's already justified us. He may discipline us, to bring us back unto Himself, and we may experience the rod of His chastisement in order that we may acknowledge our great need for Him, but never again do we fear Father's judgment.

"Most assuredly, I say to you, he who hears My word and believes in Him who sent Me has everlasting life, and shall not come into judgment, but has passed from death into life. John 5:24 NKJV

For there is one God and one Mediator between God and men, the Man Christ Jesus 1Timothy 2:5 NKJV

I do not frustrate the grace of God: for if righteousness comes by the law, then Christ is dead in vain" (Gal. 2:21).

"But that no man is justified by the law in the sight of God, it is evident: for, The just shall live by faith" (Gal. 3: 11).

To that prodigal remnant; scattered and torn, my earnest prayer is that throughout the pages of this book, you've realized that His door is always open for your return, for once we have entered the door leading to the household of faith, we eternally remain a child of God; a wayward child, perhaps, but unmistakably and undeniably His very own.

We are all God's creation but unfortunately not all of us are His children until we enter through, Jesus the door.

"To all who did receive him, to those who believed in his name, he gave the right to become children of God" (John 1:12).

Law vs. grace:

God gave us a mirror (the law..aka ten commandments)) to show us how desperately dirty we were. That mirror was never intended to clean us up, nor would it ever have the power to do so, for only the door to God's grace, (Jesus Christ) accomplished that.

Christ fulfilled the Law on our behalf and only the power of the Holy Spirit, motivating a regenerated heart can truly live in obedience. (Matthew 3:8; Acts 1:8; 1 Thessalonians 1:5; 2 Timothy 1:14).
Therefore, good works follow salvation; my friend, they do not precede it.

Those who claim righteousness on the basis of keeping the Law are unfortunately deceived and delusional

By works of the law, no one will be justified. (Galatians 2:16)

I pray that as you gaze at the beauty and grace of that open door, you will embrace the truth and allow that truth to set you free, because just as we had no say in our natural birth, we cannot secure for ourselves a place in God's family by good works or deeds. Only God has the right to permanently secure our citizenship into His kingdom, embracing us forever as sons and daughters the moment we believe.

You have two options:

You can walk back through the Door to the warm embrace of our Savior, or walk back into the darkness of Satan's tormenting domain. The choice is entirely up to you, life or death. The Bible is good news for us but if we deny it, it's a given that it'll be bad news. God left that choice to us, but the single most importance in our journey will be our perception of God. If that's perception is inaccurate, we're doomed. So it is to our eternal benefit to find out who He really is! I will be praying for you to make the right choice. If we reject our opportunity for salvation here on earth, it is written, that there will never be another. It is finished…. eternally.

I do not frustrate the grace of God: for if righteousness come by the law, then Christ is dead in vain" (Gal. 2:21).

"But that no man is justified by the law in the sight of God, it is evident: for, The just shall live by faith" (Gal. 3: 11).

Chapter Twenty:

A Galilean wedding

Over the five decades I've attended various churches, not once do I remember anything about a Galilean wedding and how it relates to the Rapture of the Bride of Christ. As first century Galileans, Jesus knew that the disciples had taken part in various weddings and would recognize immediately what He was attempting to communicate. One of the methods Jesus employed in communicating His message was through parables, and with great effectiveness. Jesus was the Master of the parable.

Long ago in Galilee, and somewhat still today, marriages were contractually pre-arranged. The Father of the groom would select the future bride for his son (usually at a very young age). The contract was signed by the parents of the bridegroom, and the bridegroom himself would pay a dowry (down payment) to the bride or her parents. This was how the marriage covenant was originally established.

Just as Jesus does not force us to accept Him as Lord and Savior when offering the gift of salvation, also the Galilean bride must first consent to the marriage, (not just because her father said so.)

The bridegroom would then offer her a ring, a gift and a drink from a cup of wine, proposing marriage. The bride would then choose to drink from that cup or refuse altogether. The covenant would be sealed if she chose to do so and they would be legally betrothed, engaged or interestingly enough; "one who was bought with a price", just as we are purchased by Christ's blood.

1 Corinthians 6:19, the apostle Paul tells us the very same thing…." Or do you not know that your body is the temple of the Holy Spirit who is

in you, whom you have from God, and you are not your own?"
Interesting parallel!

Then the groom would tell his bride, "I shall not drink from the fruit of the vine, until I drink it with you, in my Father's house." Sound familiar? -----They understood this precise phase from a traditional wedding because it embodied a common union between two parties, which is where we get the word, "communion."

The bridegroom would then return to His Father's house during that year to add a room to prepare a place for them. (My Father's house has many rooms; if that were not so, would I have told you that I am going there to prepare a place for you? And if I go and prepare a place for you, I will come back and take you to be with me that you also may be where I am. (John 14:2-3)

In the ancient culture, a father's house was where the extended family lived, a place of permanent dwelling. In Jesus's time families usually lived in clusters of buildings called, insula's. Rooms were often added on as the family grew through birth and marriage and as sons were married they were usually added to the "insula..'

To be part of the wedding feast, you had to first invited. As it is in the Galilee Wedding parallel where the father chooses the bride for his son. God does the choosing. Christ does not give the proposal. It is God who chooses the person, and gives them to Christ (Jn. 6:39).

Christ symbolizes the bridegroom of the Church (Mat. 9:15; Mk 2:20). Just like in today's culture, the bride would be busy purchasing items to assemble her wedding dress and prepare for the arrival of her groom as she saw the day approaching. Uncertain of his arrival date, she would need to be prepared, and her bridesmaids (usually under the same roof), assisted in the preparation, often pursuing the finest portions of fabrics for her dress.

Neither the bride or groom would not know what day or hour the wedding would occur. Sound familiar? Jesus also told us that, "no man knows the day or hour when He comes to rapture His bride."

When the wedding chamber was complete, the Father of the Groom would (usually in the middle of the night) proclaim the long-awaited news." Son, it's time to go get your bride." Goosebumps!!

Assembling a lighted procession throughout the streets of the city, the Bridegroom would blow the shofar, (a trumpet like rams' horn) to awaken the community to join him outside, as part of the wedding ceremony.

Once the Bridesmaids heard the shofar, they would make sure they had enough oil in their lamps, rouse the Bride, and promptly utilize their lanterns to illuminate the path to the father's house. Just as the archangel is soon to blow the trumpet in the cataclysmic event called the Rapture, the parallel is clear.

When that long awaited moment finally arrived for the betrothed, the Bridegroom would draw near his bride and beckon for her to sit upon a chair where she would be lifted up (raptured) and carried to the wedding chamber for seven days…. A parallel to the church being in heaven for seven years during the Tribulation.

The door to the wedding would be shut and any late comers turned away. When Jesus was telling his disciples this story, they realized that Jesus was the Groom and would be leaving, that the bride price would indeed be paid and that sometime in the future He would be reunited with the Bride (the church.)..

In the Bible, Jesus would reveal to His disciples that He was the Passover lamb that would be sacrificed for the sins of the world. Matthew 26:29 Jesus told His disciples, "I tell you; I will not drink of this fruit of the vine from now on until that day when I drink it anew with you in My Father's kingdom."

They understood this precise phase from a traditional wedding because it symbolized a common union between two parties, which is where we get the word, "communion. "Also, in the first miracle Jesus performed, take note that it was on the THIRD DAY...John 2:1 On the third day there was a wedding in Cana of Galilee. Remember: Christ was always accompanied by his disciples when he went to this wedding the "wine running out" refers to the animal sacrifices coming to an end, and the new wine characterized the covenant that the Bride of Christ would partake of in the New Covenant.

In Matthew 24:36, the disciples asked Jesus how the end of the age would come and what would the signs be...
36 "But of that day and hour no one knows, not even the angels of heaven, but My Father only."
Getting the picture?

Contrary to doctrinal religious views surrounding the eternal security of the believer, Jesus Christ never leaves His Bride, ever performing His sacred work of redemption from the inside out, patiently waiting until we arrive at that blessed dead end and finally recognize the engagement.

Only when we arrive at that place where we able to discern the Groom's gentle knock. Sadly, because the majority of us failed to receive discipling in our spiritual walks, we haven't a clue what the knock is or even how to access it.

Because most prodigals profoundly lack understanding of Christ's enduring faithfulness and because of the clergy's endorsement of the potential loss of salvation, prodigals can't help but remain baffled.

Just because we have chosen by an act of our own wills to remove ourselves from Father's gates of protection, whether consciously or subconsciously doesn't negate the fact that our true inheritance lies within those walls. Just because we've subjected ourselves to a harsh land, doesn't change the fact that Jesus Christ bridged our entrance into that kingdom at the moment of salvation.

It is just outside those city walls, that the enemy seductively beckons, tempting the Bride to follow his subtle suggestions. How could any of us have known that the further away we travel, the less likely we'd hear the knock or for that matter... ever return alive?

Unfortunately, many traditional churches neglect to teach us that the covenant of eternal security is, was and always will be the Father's covenant to His Son, and the Son's covenant to His Father!

Despite our best efforts we don't have the power to keep that covenant. It's Jesus' promise to the Father that: He wouldn't lose a single one of us.

When I learned the startling facts about my true citizenship and spiritual inheritance, it seemed almost ludicrous that Father would even

still care. I'd become so filthy in this world's pigpen that no one would have guessed that I was born from a royal lineage. That was precisely the enemy's plan....
Only this time....it failed.

My physical attire mattered very little to our Father, who had long ago clothed me in Christ's righteousness. Despite my false belief that I'd forfeited my salvation, Father patiently waited for that blessed moment in time when my heart cried out to Him in defeat. As He ran down that long road to meet me, He was carrying the same coat He clothed my shame in at salvation., only then would I realize that it was not even my coat to keep "clean." That coat belonged to His own dear Son and it was still perfect.

During my tragic years of wandering, I should've died and am painstakingly aware of how many of us have gone on to physical deaths only to find themselves immediately in the presence of the One who bore the guilt and shame they tried so hard to run from.

I am alive to proclaim to the prodigal who only" thinks" he has forfeited his birthright that Jesus Christ still proudly holds the title deed to that land and stands ready to deliver it.

I know that it doesn't make sense that we've traveled so far yet remain so treasured in the Father's eyes, how great the Father's love for us that we would be called sons and daughters of the Most High God. Despite our disobedience Jesus Christ secured our betrothal and the moment we said, "I do", we became engaged and sealed by His Holy Spirit.

Our Father never annuls the marriage covenant to His redeemed bride; He simply waits until we can clearly read the print for ourselves.

Further and further away some of us travel from that bold print, until its redeeming promise is no longer legible, but the fact that we moved further away will never erase the security of Christ's blood covenant.

Father, the hour has come. Glorify Your Son, that Your Son also may glorify You; And now, O Father, glorify Me together with Yourself, with the glory which I had with You before the world was" (John 17:1–5 NKJV).

The covenant of redemption was an agreement that involved both responsibility and compensation. The Son entered into a sacred agreement with the Father Submitting Himself to the functions of that covenantal agreement. An obligation was likewise assumed by the Father to reward Jesus for fulfilling the work of redemption…. the bride is His reward!

*God isn't interested in our programs or formulas to reach the sinner, let sin itself reach the sinner and simply make ourselves available to he who is hungry and invite them to the wedding supper of the Lamb.. •

Chapter Twenty-One:

Claiming the spoils

Despite the crippling pain of arthritis, it was Grandma's nightly custom to drop to her knees and pray with her bedroom door wide open; her voice just audible enough, that from my bedroom across the hall, I could detect tidbits of her lengthy conversations with God.

Although I found it a bit strange that she kept her door open, Grandma displayed not even the slightest hint of embarrassment. Those lengthy prayers brought me such distress that I'd often get up and close my door, angry at the audacity she displayed in conferring aloud with God about my life, when I wasn't the least bit interested in His opinion.

Yet that image of Grandma on her knees eventually made its way beyond the internal noise of my troubled soul, searing its imprint exactly where God ordained... in the deepest recesses of my heart.

As a young child, I was mortified of entering Grandma's room. The aura of peace radiating from that atmosphere flickered the essence of a holy God I felt sure hated me and desired only my demise. I was certain that if I allowed this God even the slightest access into my world of confusion and pain, He'd be sure to see the real me and broadcast what a miserable disappointment I was to the world. So very little did I know.

If I entered her room for whatever reason, I'd hastily make my way back out because above her bed, hung a picture of Jesus, His eyes seemingly following my every step, condemning and judging my sin, scorning the shame that had become my daily companion. And although I had indeed accepted Jesus Christ at the age of eleven, my perception of His character was sorely altered due to the faulty doctrine and sexual abuse received at an earlier age.

Sovereign words were spoken in that room concerning my life, conversations that only Grandma and God were privy to. Although many years would pass before those words materialized, they would indeed manifest at the appropriate time and season, simply because of God's faithfulness to perform His Word.

Grandma remained diligent on my behalf, faithful to the burden entrusted to her. She never preached at me and I don't recall even one instance when she became angry with me despite the numerous opportunities provided her.

She lived her life solely to the glory of her invisible King, caring not who was watching or what their opinion might be, seizing every earthly opportunity to interject a valuable parable or two into my life. Oblivious to my verbal protests that "religion" was slowly capturing her mind.

Occasionally she'd ask me to just sit and brush her hair, or just talk awhile, and I'd oblige, only under the strict condition that she refrain from her incessant obsession of talking about Jesus.

Grandma would graciously accept my offer, and anxiously pull up a chair for both of us to sit down. Her cheeks donning a familiar radiance, she'd joyfully initiate the conversation, careful to stay within the boundaries of our spoken agreement, yet it wouldn't be long before she'd begin rambling on about people I'd never heard of, speaking about these foreigners as though we were personally related. Abraham, Isaac, and Jacob; just to name a few, and of course, we can't forget Moses, Elijah and the Israelites, to whom I hadn't a clue. However, bound to the terms of our agreement, I'd sit and listen, thinking smugly to myself, "Who in the world would ever name a child that?"

Grandma was simply planting seeds in the weeded garden of my soul. She cared not what my response was, nor did she take offense at my obvious rebellion, she simply obeyed and trusted her Savior for the outcome.
She invested her life in that trusted seed, understanding how very limited her time was with a keener awareness of the future harvest.

The hidden hope and substance of my calling had been long ago fashioned in Grandma's quiet place by God and though He understood completely what I'd have to go through to finally cross over into its fullness, I'm sure Grandma didn't have a clue to the vast scope and nature of the burden she carried, or that her obedience would one day encompass the sovereign release of an entire remnant of prodigals just like me.

Her obedience in yielding to that urgency was an accomplishment greatly to be honored, because though she believed she was petitioning heaven for only one; in actuality her burden was for each and every prodigal that would one day read this book.

Long before I ever agreed to do so, our Father preordained that this prodigal daughter would effectively deliver the spiritual truths contained in this book and unmask the enemy who so desperately sought my destruction. My faith has withstood untold trials that I might effectively declare the covenant Jesus Christ made with His Father…that I may one day, without reservation, deliver this message of eternal security; proclaiming the truth that: no man has the power to take the gift of eternal security from us and that none of His sheep will remain lost; regardless of present-day location.

Grandma Myrna went home to be with our Groom in the winter of 1993, her long awaited home in glory awaiting; the invisible, eternal mansion that, as a child, I questioned and even mocked.

Peeking through Heaven's glorious portals, I envision Grandma joyfully beholding her long-awaited harvest, smiling as each prodigal runs through the Door (Jesus) into Father's awaiting arms. God, in His infinite mercy knew that only a perfect, blameless sacrifice would suffice for this entire human race, so He opened the only Door in all of eternity capable of meeting His requirement for perfection.

The curtain of flesh preventing us from beholding our holy God was ripped, once and for all when Jesus Christ said," it is finished, "that we may behold Him forever. God the Father will never retract or erase His completed work, despite man's doctrinal interpretations to the contrary.

Promise me that when you've grasped the truth within these pages, you'll learn how to share it. This world's far too vast for one man to reach alone, yet our enemy lives and breathes

to prevent this world from discovering that one Man has indeed victoriously reached it….
The Man, Jesus Christ.

 **"Consequently, he is able to save to the uttermost those who draw near to God through him, since he always lives to make intercession for them.
"Hebrews 7:2**

Chapter Twenty-Two:
The Rapture

Looking back over the past year, 2020, it's obvious that the whole world is going through undeniable changes. To believe the lie that all this will settle down and go back to whatever "normal" is supposed to be is just wishful thinking.

Matthew 24, Luke 21, and 2 Timothy 3 provide us with critical end-time markers. Many Christians believe that we are in the "end-times" and that Christ's return is imminent. We are witnessing earthquakes, global weather pattern changes, famine, and war on the news daily. Is this the end of the" church age of grace" signaling Christ's return?

Natural disasters have always been in the media, but are now occurring at" warp speed." Books such as the" Left Behind series" depicts that monumental day when all of Christ's *followers, the" Body of Christ" will disappear, and in the" twinkling of an eye "be removed from earth physically in the event known as the rapture—while the others are left behind to survive the seven-year tribulation on earth.*

The Greek word used to describe rapture is harpazo, it means "to be caught up, to snatch away", as seen in 1 Thessalonians 4:17 (NASB)

Even Christians are beginning to question their faith trying to make sense of the sudden destruction and loss from COVID-19..
Suffering citizens are seeking answers to their personal experiences with many turning to substance abuse, "new age" philosophies and suicide. Satan is convincing many that everything is "normal" and that the problem lies with us, the believers....(scoffers will scoff. Haters will hate!)

He is preparing the way for the ultimate evil antichrist and false prophet to appear. Sadly, a majority of the earth's population will fall prey to being

seduced by their doctrines. Christians are being labeled as "haters," and

the persecution (as the Bible states) is just beginning.

FYI…

Life will not continue as before; ever!!

Satanic influence is obvious, and his followers are on task. For believers, this is a sign how very close we are to experiencing the rapture of the church, bringing an end to the dispensation of grace. Jesus said we would know the season and the season has arrived. Therefore, my question to you is: If not now, when?

After the Rapture, it will be still be possible for people to be saved but the Bible warns that Christians will be beheaded for their faith.

Revelation 6:9-11 illustrates exactly what happens to those killed during the tribulation, however to avoid the wrath of the tribulation altogether would be the wisest choice you could ever make.

Are you willing to gamble that Jesus won't come today? Satan would love for you to embrace that dumb lie but Jesus promised that we would be raptured in the twinkling of an eye. Being prepared beforehand is highly advisable.

The rapture is an event where Jesus Christ will appear in the air, the trumpet will sound, and all believers in Christ will leave this planet. Those who have died since the resurrection of Christ receive their resurrected bodies. Those that are alive will also be changed in the twinkling of an eye and depart this world.

The most vivid description of this event is found in 1 Thessalonians 4:16-18, "For the Lord himself shall descend from heaven with a shout, with the voice of the archangel, and with the trump of God: and the dead in Christ shall rise first: Then we which are alive and remain shall be caught up together with them in the clouds, to meet the Lord in the air: and so shall we ever be with the Lord. Wherefore comfort one another with these words." see also 1 Corinthians 15:50-58.

This event leaves on earth everyone who does not know Christ as their Lord and Savior. Following the rapture is a short transition period. The Antichrist will then sign a seven-year treaty (covenant) with many nations concerning the city of Jerusalem beginning the seven-year tribulation period (Daniel 9:27).
As promised in 1Thessaloniansv1:9-10, the Bride of Christ will not see the wrath of God as we are raptured before the tribulation. Revelation 3:10, "Because thou hast kept the word of my patience, I also will keep thee from the hour of temptation, which shall come upon all the world, to try them that dwell upon the earth."

After the third chapter of Revelation, the church is gone until Revelation chapter 19 when she returns as the Bride of Christ.

It would take more than time permits to make a comprehensive study of the chronological order of the rapture and future events. However, as of right now, Christians are still on Earth and the Tribulation has not yet begun....

Please allow your decision to be an educated one.

God certainly didn't require me to walk back into the enemy's camp, I willingly and joyfully volunteered, because with great knowledge comes even greater responsibility. If you have read this book in its entirety, you've been informed of the facts surrounding this confusing spiritual war.

The choice is now up to you to choose to live abundantly, escaping the enemy's fierce grip or to forget what you've read and go on with your captivity.

Whatever your choice, God wants you to know that He loves you beyond anything you could dare imagine and that the enemy's pathetic lies will always seek to deter and confuse.

Had my physical life been destroyed in this war, I obviously wouldn't be testifying to the fact that Jesus Christ came to destroy the works of the devil. As I've stated, many of my friends didn't live to escape the frightening power behind their darkness. I pray that somehow, my testimony effectively reaches even one confused and wayward soul to see the Light.

The longer a prodigal remains in darkness, the less light he sees. The more he sins, while reaping the resulting consequences of his sin, the darker life appears to him, altering his perceptions and changing his beliefs.

In order for the prodigal to clearly see Jesus Christ, they must first behold the enemy and appreciate that eternal life is just that.....eternal. I promised Father that, for as long as He allowed me breath, I would continue to share the many wonders of His love, demonstrating the truth of His character to the best of my ability.

My declaration of Independence will remain upon earth as carefully crafted evidence, testifying to the wonder working power of the cross, reflecting God's enormous window of grace, that His prodigals might glance through and find His Majesty waiting with arms stretched open wide.

Despite the long and tedious challenges, we encounter along the way, despite the hopelessness of our situations, we will stand, as trophies of grace in the Father's hand.
Of all the things I've lost in this life, I'm grateful that salvation was never, nor could it ever be one of them, for my beloved Savior promised, that" My Father, who has given them to Me, is greater than all; and no one is able to snatch them out of My Father's hand. John 10:29 NKJV

That the saying might be fulfilled which He spoke, "Of those whom You gave Me I have lost none." John 19:9

Disclaimer:

I wish to state for the reader's curiosity that I do not affiliate myself with any particular denomination, religious affiliation, or recovery program; simply as a redeemed member of the body of Christ, a daughter of Almighty God.

When I make reference to God; I am referring to the God of the scriptures; the God of Abraham, Isaac and Jacob; the God of my forefathers, and not an abstract deity formulated in my imagination, conjured up by a carnal mind.

When I refer to salvation, I am referring to the spiritual act of becoming, "born again", not of the flesh- as in our first birth but of God's own Spirit, through His Son, Jesus Christ, this world's only true Savior.

When I make reference to spirit in lower case, I am referring to the literal and actual spirit indwelling every human being.

When the "S" is capitalized, I am always referring to the Holy Spirit indwelling only those having become children of God, the only humans enlightened and empowered at the moment of salvation with the full counsel of God, who alone is able to illuminate and integrate divine perception into the soul.

Without the Holy Spirit indwelling the human spirit NONE of us are capable of changing our nature, yet every true child of God possesses the supernatural ability to overthrow the soul's old order with its egotistical rules and selfish ambitions to enter into the promised land where dreams really do come true and Daddy really does love His children.

I survived only because of Christ's covenant with the Father on my behalf, not what I did or didn't do.

My prayer is that I have succeeded in delivering this message as accurately and as powerfully as I have interpreted it from the Holy Spirit. I wear no labels; neither do I profess my sin to be a residual byproduct of any particular disease that I'm "recovering" from. There was nothing worthy in me to begin with that by "recovering" I could possibly return to ...nothing at all. I was; as we all are born into a condition called sin of which I had absolutely no control over, then born again into a condition called righteousness of which Jesus Christ...and He alone obtained. My name is Merry Jo and I am, was and always will be a daughter of the living God, called by His name, alive solely for His glory.

10 The thief cometh not, but for to steal, and to kill, and to destroy: I am come that they might have life, and that they might have it more abundantly.

11 I am the good shepherd: the good shepherd giveth his life for the sheep.

Epilogue:

Left behind

To the scoffers,

I advise you to store this letter safely so that you can refer to it after the Rapture. Please know that if you are left behind, living in the Great Tribulation period, you WILL have the opportunity to accept Jesus Christ, but will be executed for doing so.

Revelation 3:10 should remove any doubt, as to what just transpired in this world...

"Because thou hast kept the word of my patience, I also will keep thee from the hour of temptation, which shall come upon all the world, to try them that dwell upon the earth."

What just occurred is that Jesus Christ has suddenly removed all born-again believers, (the true Church) from this planet in a foretold event

called The Rapture. The best description of this event is found in 1 Thessalonians 4:16-18, "For the Lord himself shall descend from heaven with a shout, with the voice of the archangel, and with the trump of God: and the dead in Christ shall rise first: Then we which are alive and remain shall be caught up together with them in the clouds, to meet the Lord in the air: and so shall we ever be with the Lord. Wherefore comfort one another with these words.
*Hopefully you will have taken heed to the warnings God has provided you prior to the Rapture but if, for whatever reason, you haven't, I want you to listen closely.....

I'm sure you're frightened and astonished at the chaos that just transpired. Millions of people have disappeared. You are perplexed and confused, wondering what the truth is..

The media (true to their nature) is portraying otherwise, hoping you'll believe that those of us removed (likely using the alien abduction theory) were defective or inferior, educating you with instructions that are meant solely for your demise.

Don't trust them!

The chaos resulting from the Rapture will be such as this world has never seen, causing a world leader called the Antichrist to jump aboard and proclaim to have "all" the answers, offering a FALSE sense of peace. He is your enemy! I repeat...this charismatic leader is nothing but a brutal dictator, ushering in the time period the Bible refers to as The Tribulation.

The world will be deceived into embracing this brilliant man as "savior," but this era will usher in unprecedented plagues, unreasonable amounts of suffering, earthquakes, famine and death.

The devil wants to be embraced as the true God, remember? He came to steal, kill and destroy, remember?

This has always been his nature, the very reason he was removed from his divine position, and the Antichrist will be the incarnation of Satan.

He will celebrate the fact that people actually worship and depend upon him as God, demanding that all remaining on the planet worship him, requiring them to take his mark of the beast in the forehead or back of the hand. If you accept this mark, you will be condemned to hell with no opportunity for repentance!

The Jews will readily embrace the Antichrist as he "appears" to bring peace in the Middle East, even decreeing a rebuilding of the Jewish Temple. He will enter the Temple in Jerusalem, offering a sacrifice that will be an abomination to the Jews and declare openly to be God. Only then will they recognize the deception, fleeing to Petra to prevent being slaughtered. Petra, meaning "Rock" in Greek, is a deserted city south of the Dead Sea in Jordan.

Satan will demand that all remaining on the planet worship him, requiring them to take the mark of the beast the forehead or back of the hand.

If you accept this mark, you will be condemned to hell with no opportunity for repentance.!

If you renounce this mark the Bible states in Revelation that you will be executed. Renounce it anyway! Spending eternity with Christ far surpasses any suffering you will endure on earth.

My prayer is that you embrace Him now to prevent separation from God eternally!!!

Hebrews 3:7
TODAY *if ye will hear his voice, harden not your hearts.*"

Pay it forward…. Foremost in the heart of God is the care of the fatherless, the widow, and the needy. Each of us will one day fall within one of those categories at some point in our lives.

While upon this earth, I may never understand God's eternal purposes in allowing the destruction in my early childhood years. What I HAVE learned through it all though is that my heavenly Father is real, that He is sovereign, and that I shall cling to His strong and mighty hand for the rest of my days.

Then, when my days upon this earth are finished, (or the Rapture occurs first) I shall see my Savior face to face, and oh, what a glorious day that shall be.

Many waters cannot quench love nor can the floods drown the incredible deliverance God places in each of our spirits at the moment of salvation.

We can rest assured that if we belong to Jesus Christ and have surrendered our lives to His sovereign care, NOTHING shall separate us from the incredible destiny awaiting us.

For I am persuaded, that neither death, nor life, nor angels, nor principalities, nor powers, nor things present, nor things to come,
Nor height, nor depth, nor any other creature, shall be able to separate us from the love of God, which is in Christ Jesus our Lord. Romans 8:38-39

More than twenty years ago, God told me that I would write a book. Its scope and content, He failed to elaborate upon, until the appointed time. God knew that it would take Him every second of those twenty years to prepare my soul for the fight that lay ahead in getting these words out to His prodigals.

Father had to skillfully prepare my unsteady hands for the war currently gripping the souls of His elect. His hands had to fashion my soul in the crucible of truth and humility that I might valiantly proclaim the truths presented throughout these pages with assurance far beyond my human understanding.

It would take Him that long to posture me, rightfully positioning my shield to skillfully withstand and oppose the fiery darts most certain to come my way, training my heart to deploy rapidly and without consequence any sting of mass destruction deployed by the enemy.

Long before I became aware of the power of the enemy in my life, our Father was carefully calculating his end. Because God grieves over how many of His prodigals still remain locked up in that house of bondage, He's carefully trained me to assist in that escape. Long before I said yes to His clever utilization of my life's torment, this battle was already in full swing. My agreement to co-labor with Him, I assure you, has only intensified this fight.

Getting this message out across enemy lines, I assure you, hasn't been easy, but I'm finally positioned for the fight. Although it's true that the *war is officially over, your enemy isn't going to bow out gracefully and accept defeat, particularly if you choose to remain blind to your inheritance.*

Our Redeemer lives. and I can promise that the moment this realization hits you, all hell will break loose.

But fear not, child of God…….

For this reason, was the Son of God manifest...

*** **TO DESTROY THE WORKS OF THE DEVIL**

1John 3:8

If the devil has ever tried to shut you up, beat you up, put a gag order on you, rest assured, beloved, your calling is tremendous. Salvation's road is indeed narrow, but once we are on it, we are ETERNALLY on it! Some of us sit down on the road and go about our daily lives, others walk backwards or sideways, while yet others rest in the bushes, hide in the alley, or stubbornly refuse to move forward on this narrow road, but we can be certain that we remain firmly fixed on salvation's road because of one reason alone…. the precious blood of Jesus Christ, this world's only Savior! Don't let anyone convince you otherwise!

God's front porch…

As I stood upon God 's front porch, the voice said, "enter in." The light inside became so brilliant, clearly exposing my guilt and sin. Looking down at my filthy garments, I turned and started to run.

I knew that I was unworthy, so ashamed of the things I'd done. Startled by His presence, there my Savior stood, I fell to my knees when I saw Him, just as I knew that anyone would. His voice was so very gentle, His eyes so full of grace. He looked at me and spoke softly, "Enter in child, your sins I've erased.".

As I stood on God's porch sobbing, it all became so clear, all that I'd learned about Him in Sunday school, yes, my Savior was finally here. As I looked back across the threshold, at the multitudes standing in line, My Heavenly Father embraced me as He welcomed me in to dine.

"Father, why is Jesus crying?"

"What has made Him grieve?"

"Where are all these people going?"

"Why must they all leave?"

His reply will forever remain embedded in my tender spirit. "Child, every sin they have ever committed, today they must each one bare it." "For them, My Son's death has been in vain; by His blood they could've been saved." "He must now say goodbye eternally to the ones who rejected His name."

"Oh Father, I'm so very grateful," I cried, "so unworthy to be in Your home." As I bowed my head in worship, I felt my tears touch His very throne. I woke up in a panic and I heard the Spirit say, 'Go tell the ones that you saw standing in line that My blood has paved the way."

"Tell them about the banquet, and how I've saved them all a seat."

"Tell them that I have paid in full, to prevent this eternal defeat."

"Tell them that I am knocking, they must soon answer the door."

"Behold I am coming quickly, and time will be no more."

Luke 13:25 but when the head of the house has locked the door, it will be too late. Then you will stand outside knocking and pleading, Lord open the door for us, but he will reply, I do not know you.

ABC's of Salvation:

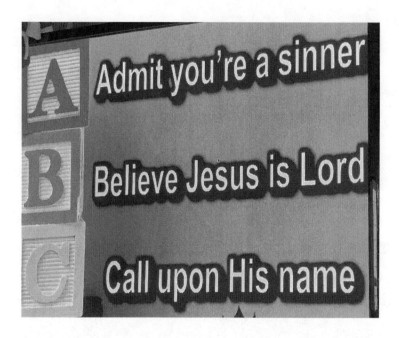

For all have sinned, and come short of the glory of God; Romans 3:23
"That if you confess with your mouth the Lord Jesus and believe in your heart that God has raised Him from the dead, you will be saved" Romans 10:9

The grace of our Lord Jesus Christ be with you all. Amen" (Rom 16:24).

Recommendations:
Tune into JD Farag's weekly (Sunday) prophecy updates on Jdfarag.org or YouTube
Farag of Calvary Chapel Kaneohe, Hawaii shares weekly Bible Prophecy Updates that cover current global events and End Times related news. His teaching will catch you up real fast! WARPSPEED!!!

Must follow YouTube channels:
Watchman on the wall 88(Chad Thomas,)
Ty Green
Pastors:Robert Breaker with his (wonder working "white board,") Tim Henderson, Billy

Crone, Andy Woods and last but not least, Chuck Missler

The true Gospel…Don't let anyone convince you otherwise! It's truly a matter of life and death!

1 Corinthians 15:

1 Moreover, brethren, I declare unto you the Gospel which I preached unto you, which you also have received, and wherein ye stand,

2 by which ye also are saved if ye keep in memory what I preached unto you— unless ye have believed in vain.

3 For I delivered unto you first of all that which I also received: how that Christ died for our sins according to the Scriptures,

4 and that He was buried, and that He arose again the third day according to the Scriptures,

~Benediction… Now may the God of peace who brought up our Lord Jesus from the dead, that great Shepherd of the sheep, through the blood of the **everlasting covenant**, make you complete in every good work to do His will, working in you what is well pleasing in His sight, through Jesus Christ, to whom be glory forever and ever. Amen. Hebrews 13:20-21NKJV~

Authors previous books:

"Behold I Stand at the Door and Knock"

My Poetic Justice

@ MJPortell.com

Made in the USA
Columbia, SC
16 February 2024